Pennsylvania LIGHTHOUSES *on* LAKE ERIE

Pennsylvania LIGHTHOUSES *on* LAKE ERIE

EUGENE H. WARE

THE History PRESS

Published by The History Press
Charleston, SC
www.historypress.net

Front cover: Presque Isle Light Station. *Author's collection. Back cover, left*: North Pierhead Light. *Courtesy of the Pennsylvania DCNR files. Back cover, right*: Erie Land Lighthouse. *Author's collection.*

First published 2016

Manufactured in the United States

ISBN 978.1.46711.874.3

Library of Congress Control Number: 2015945696

CONTENTS

PREFACE

The first known light beacon in the world, the Pharos of Alexandria, was located on an island at the head of the harbor to the port of Alexandria, Egypt. Pharos was originally lit sometime in 250 BC, after more than twenty years of construction. Greek architect Sostratus of Gnidus was in charge of designing and building this massive structure, the base and first two floors of which measured 98 feet square. A central light tower rose an additional 367 feet. Alexander the Great built the structure in the city he named for himself, and it was said to have cost over 267 tons of silver.

The Pharos was in full-time use until AD 641, when Islamic warriors conquered Alexandria and caused serious damage to the light and building during their long siege. That means the building, at that point, had been in service for an unimaginable ten centuries. While it was not in use the entire time, it actually survived for an additional five hundred years until it was finally destroyed by a series of earthquakes in the fourteenth century. Today, Pharos is recognized as one of the Seven Wonders of the Ancient World.

Before Pharos, the first lighting systems were designed to help mariners by providing early warning of submerged rocks, reefs, cliffs and sandbars where ships could run aground. They were also used to help alert ships of other coastal hazards. Most were very primitive methods, such as fires on the cliffs or beaches. Two huge problems with these fires were the vast supply of wood that was always necessary and the fact that the fires had to be constantly watched and supervised. It was not long before the builders of these fire-based lights realized that by elevating these fires,

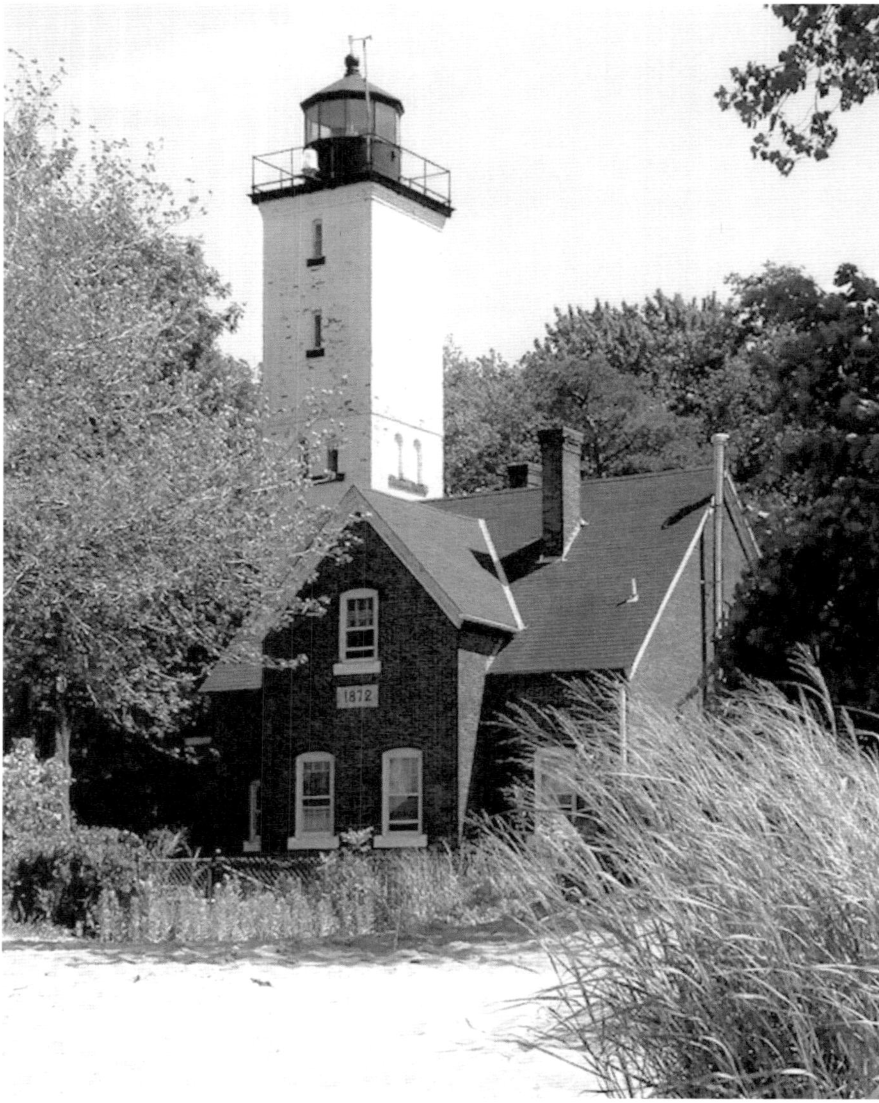

A close-up view of Presque Isle Light Station in 2004. *Author's collection.*

they could be seen farther out at sea. Thus began the world's recognition of the lighthouse.

From the beginning, sailors have had a particular need for light. They recognized that the hazards of navigation were challenging enough in calm and daylight situations, but when night and severe weather worked together to create low visibility, navigation at sea could become all but impossible. As the world's nations began to use the seas to trade, the need for navigation aids such as lighthouses increased tremendously.

Once Spain, England, France and Holland all began to establish colonies and settlements in North and South America, shipping and trading grew at rapid rates. The need for more lighthouses, especially on the North American shores, quickly became evident. However, it was in the Caribbean, where the Spanish had an enormous influence, that the first lighthouse in the New World was built. It was constructed and opened in 1563 on the island of Cuba on the shores at Havana. It was named the Morro Light of Havana.

The first lighthouse in North America was authorized by an act of the English assembly and built by the Massachusetts Bay Colony at the entrance to the harbor of Boston in 1716. This lighthouse sits on Little Brewster Island, about eight miles from Boston, and has been designated a National Historic Landmark. During the Revolutionary War, the British destroyed part of it, but it was rebuilt with a new eighty-nine-foot tower in 1873. Records indicate that there were only seventy lighthouses in the world during those early years. A dozen or so of them were on the Atlantic coast of North America. Today, this lighthouse, known as the Boston Light, is the only light still manned by resident keepers. The light is serviced today by three active-duty U.S. Coast Guardsmen, and all hold the designation of lighthouse keeper. As a gesture of respect for a very old and venerable occupation, the Boston Light continues this worthy tradition of service.

For the next one hundred years, many new lighthouses dotted the coastlines of Canada, the English colonies and, finally, the new United States of America. Wherever ships ventured, the need for a lighthouse soon followed. The English colonists and colonies led the way in lighthouse construction along the eastern coast of North America. Soon after the American Revolution, individual states assumed responsibility for the lighthouses in their areas.

However, in August 1789, one of the first acts of the newly formed United States Congress was to assume the responsibility for all navigation aids within the new nation. It has been said that this act was passed due almost entirely to pressure from President George Washington. Washington, once a surveyor by trade, wanted to have the ability to appoint lighthouse keepers, negotiate with contractors and supervise the building of any new lighthouses. Both John Adams and Thomas Jefferson, the next two presidents, also carried on this tradition. The first two lighthouses built under this legislation were Maine's Portland Head Light and the Old Cape Henry Light in Chesapeake

Bay. These lighthouses were built under President Washington's direct supervision. He also appointed the keepers of both lights and continued these practices for seven additional lights in the following years.

During the early years, all lighthouses were officially placed under the Department of the Treasury. Much like what sometimes happens today, a department that is assigned a particular duty by an act of Congress may be unprepared and unwilling to take responsibility for the management of its new duties. When this delegation of lighthouses responsibility came about, it was a total surprise to the Department of the Treasury. Within the department, the responsibilities and management of this new area became like a ping-pong ball and bounced all over its various internal offices.

Finally in 1820, the responsibility for all the lighthouses was given to Stephen Pleasonton, a fifth auditor within the Department of the Treasury. Even back in the early days of the republic, the audit area of this department was widely known for passing paper from desk to desk and getting little accomplished. Pleasonton, who was a passionate bean counter, was given the title of general superintendent of lights. He was a bookkeeper and had no experience in any of the fields related to his new duties.

All knew him as the perfect practicing bureaucrat. Right from the start, Pleasonton failed to realize his real duty involved the lives and safety of the ships, crews and passengers. His actual responsibility was to provide all of them with the best navigation aids possible, and cost should have been a secondary issue. Unfortunately, during the time he held this position, his only focus was on economy and never on quality or safety.

A strange but true fact about Pleasonton is that some held him in hero status for something he had done many years before. In his early years, he was recognized as a very somber and serious young man who happened to be born the same year as his beloved nation. By a simple act, he would become a dashing war hero in the War of 1812. It was because of his quick actions that he single-handedly saved the original Declaration of Independence. As the British were advancing on Washington, D.C., in 1814, the secretary of state asked him to move many of the State Department records to a safer location. Pleasonton quickly made arrangements to purchase large bolts of linen and had the cloth made into crude bags. Throwing as many documents as he could into the bags, he loaded them all into a cart and drove them to Leesburg, Virginia, about thirty miles from Washington. Included in these bags were the Declaration of Independence, the official journals of Congress and Washington's notes and correspondences. It was not until the next morning—after what he called a wonderful sleep following too much work—that he realized the British had indeed burned the White House, the Capitol, the treasury and nearly every other important building in the Washington area. By 10:00 a.m., the State Department building was nothing more than smoking rubble. The only records that survived were what Pleasonton was able to remove.

In spite of this, when he took over as the superintendent of lights, he became even better known for his penny-pinching policies and a huge number of glaring irregularities, shady transactions and self-dealings that took place during his management. Historians consider his service as superintendent to be the low point in American lighthouse history. During this service, there were times when Congress and the presidents either told him to stop doing something or informed him that he needed to accomplish a particular task, and Pleasonton simply took it upon himself to ignore them. Ultimately, he was removed from office, but only after thirty-two years in the position.

In 1873, George H. Elliot, major of engineers and the engineering secretary of the United States Lighthouse Board, said:

> *It is not alone in view of its economic effects that the lighthouse system is to be regarded. It is a life-preserving establishment, founded on the principals* [sic] *of Christian benevolence…A failure of such a light to send forth its expected ray is, as it were, a breach of solemn promise, which may allure the confiding mariner to an untimely death or disastrous shipwreck.*

This and the fact that the U.S. Lighthouse Service was in the process of publishing what was to become, and still is, the bible for light keepers, called *Instructions to the Employees of the United States Lighthouse Service*, showed exactly how serious the federal government had become about the proper administration of the nation's lighthouses.

Sometime around 1781, the lighting of the inland sea, more commonly known as the Great Lakes, was begun in North America. The first attempt at establishing a lighthouse on the Great Lakes was the building of a signal fire in a lantern room of the British Fort Niagara. The fire was on the roof of the fort that was located at the mouth of the Niagara River on Lake Ontario. This makeshift light—erected soon after the HMS *Ontario* sank in October 1780 after it left the fort at Oswego, New York, in a violent gale—provided some help for ships in the area. British records show that over eighty people who were aboard the *Ontario* perished that evening when it sank.

This mishap demonstrated to both the Americans and the British Canadians the power of the Great Lakes and how these lakes could be more punishing on ships than many of the world's oceans. Back in the 1700s and 1800s, Great Lakes sailors quickly learned that the wind and waves on the lakes could ramp up quickly and horrific thunderstorms could develop. Many told their superiors that the lakes made them feel like they were ensnared in a typical ocean storm.

With its nearly perfect east–west axis, Lake Erie can produce its special brand of nasty weather. During certain times of the year, the lake is inclined to develop lake-effect weather that can become thunderstorms and winter blizzards. This particular type of weather pattern has a bad habit of coming up silently and quickly and has always had a serious effect on sailors on the lake. The winds coming in off the lake can become exceedingly high and can produce dangerous and even deadly results. Information about the weather near the port of Erie and on Lakes Erie and Ontario will be covered in more detail in Chapter 2.

When the American Revolution finally ended in 1783, the treaties set the southern British Canadian borders approximately through the middle of the Great Lakes, except for Lake Michigan, which was entirely within the United States. This fact meant that both countries had shorelines on all the other lakes.

Both the United States and Canada soon realized that the Great Lakes would need more lighthouses to protect people, cargo and vessels, and both nations pledged to accomplish this goal. However, it would not be until 1796, fully thirteen years after the signing of the treaties, that Canada and Britain finally turned the military garrison at Niagara over to the United States. Most citizens of the Great Lakes area viewed the British delays at Niagara and the non-action of the American government as a perilous assessment of the real value of the hard-fought Revolutionary War. Unquestionably, this observation proved to be true. To irrevocably win freedom from British influence and control, the United States would be required to fight and win the War of 1812. This is commonly known as the Second War for Independence.

Once the United States did gain control of the lighthouse at Niagara, it did not take long for it to be deactivated as a working aid to navigation by the new government in Washington. By the time 1800 arrived, one of the early actions that year was to have the wooden tower torn down. The new nation, totally controlled by political bosses in the East—mainly in Boston, Washington and Philadelphia—had little or no interest in expanding the nation's borders to the west. Only the eastern coastal areas were of real interest to these leaders. It was not until twenty-three turbulent years later and five administration changes in Washington that finally, in 1823, a new wooden lighthouse was built atop the old fort.

In 1805, Congress did authorize the building of a lighthouse at the port of Buffalo, New York, but government officials refused to adopt funding for construction or operation of the light. To correct this problem, in 1810, a newly elected Congress authorized construction and approved funding for two light stations on Lake Erie. The original one at Buffalo, New York, plus another one at Presque Isle, Erie, Pennsylvania, were both authorized. Unfortunately, the War of 1812 intervened, and all the funds set aside for the lights and the men to build them were instead diverted to building Oliver Hazard Perry's Lake Erie fleet within the sheltered harbor at Erie. It was not until 1817 that the lighthouse plans were revisited, and in 1818, that construction was able to begin on these lighthouses.

Both of these lights opened in 1819, within a few days of each other. The Presque Isle Light, located on the high cliff along Erie's east side, was the earliest American lighthouse to display a light on the Great Lakes. Although there is some contention about which was the first, most historians agree that the two were the first actual lighthouses to open on the Great Lakes. Even though there were a few wooden towers before this, these towers were never considered actual lighthouses. The first lighthouse keeper at the original Presque Isle Light was an Erie native, Captain John Bone, who moved his wife and six children into the small house on the grounds one week later.

This is where the story about the three lighthouses at Erie, Pennsylvania, begins. For reasons many people cannot explain, a lighthouse is thought to be a unique tonic for mind, body and soul. It seems it has some magical power and nearly universal appeal. Maybe it's the fact that a certain

MOVING AHEAD

A new nine-member lighthouse board replaced Pleasonton in 1852 and is credited with making vast progress. In 1910, Congress decided to streamline the system by creating the Bureau of Lighthouses. With this move, they appointed a manager and cut back on the military involvement in lighthouse activity. Finally, in 1939, the U.S. Coast Guard adopted all U.S. lighthouses and is still the official custodian of most of them today.

charm is represented by the purely imaginary life of the lighthouse keeper. Nothing moves the imagination quite like this fictional dream of lighthouses and their keepers' way of life. As you will see within the pages of this book, the fantasy life imagined by many of the lighthouse keepers is far from the actual truth.

1

A SHORT HISTORY OF THE PORT OF ERIE

In a strange twist of fate, Lake Erie, which was to become the water superhighway to the west, was the last of the Great Lakes to be discovered by the European colonists. In 1615, French explorer Samuel de Champlain used Indians to lead his contingent up the St. Lawrence River as far as Montreal. From there, they went up the Ottawa River and continued west by using other waterways in Canada. Eventually, they went down the French River to Georgian Bay, which led them into Lake Huron. Because of its very northerly course, this route was only usable seven months of the year due to ice on the waterways. This path was very long and would completely bypass both Lake Ontario and Lake Erie. Lake Erie was ultimately discovered in 1669, over fifty years later.

The story of Erie, its harbor and, eventually, its three lighthouses begins back in 1679, when Robert de La Salle, a French explorer, built and launched the first sail vessel on Lake Erie, *Le Griffon*. He built this little ship in the stark wilderness rather than a shipyard, in a sheltered cove along the Niagara River scarcely three miles above the falls. The ship was built and designed like a ship-of-war, although La Salle meant it to be nothing more than a supply ship to sail the waters of Lake Erie and beyond. Its maiden voyage left Niagara on August 7, 1679, with a crew and passengers numbering sixteen. It sailed the length of Lake Erie to present-day Detroit. From there, it sailed on to Green Bay on Lake Michigan. On September 18, 1679, La Salle issued orders that dispatched a crew of six to sail back to Niagara with a full load of furs. He had traded with the Indians of the area to get the furs

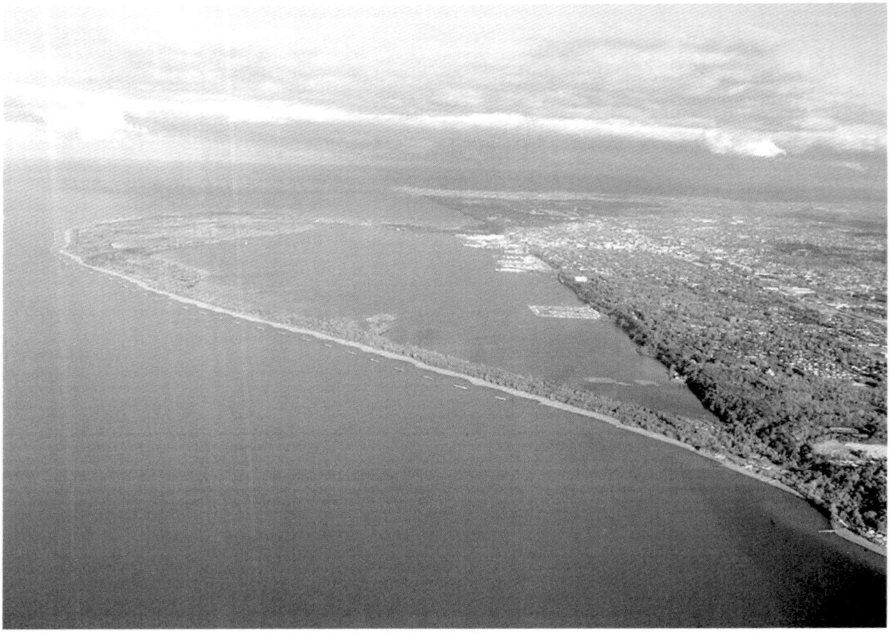

An aerial view of Presque Isle State Park. *Courtesy of the Pennsylvania DCNR files.*

and then returned to Green Bay to pick up supplies before sailing. Once the ship left, it was never seen again.

Early on in the history of Erie, the strategic and geographic importance of this small corner of Lake Erie, midway between Buffalo and Cleveland, began to be well known by both the French Canadians and the British colonists. During most of the 1750s, the British and French were embroiled in what was virtually a worldwide war. Part of this war was entangled with claims by both sides of ownership of the areas around the Great Lakes, plus much of the Ohio and Mississippi River Valleys. The French invasion of this and other areas, including parts of Ohio, was only part of a sequence of events leading to a world war, known in America as the French and Indian War and in Europe as the Seven Years' War.

In October 1752, during this ongoing struggle with the English for dominance and possession of the Great Lakes region, the Frenchman Marquis Duquesne became the governor of Canada or, as some called it, New France. Shortly after this appointment, he secured the services of a few younger French military explorers: Chevalier Pierre-Paul Marin, Michel Jean Hughes Pean and Chevalier Le Mercier. In the beginning, all reported to a young adventurer named Charles Deschamps de Boishébert. Before long, the job started to seem too much for the young de Boishébert. Duquesne's only choice was to turn the total leadership for the mission over to Paul Marin, a much more experienced explorer. Marin and the two others were put in charge of building a French fort on the banks of Lake Erie, plus two or more inland on the route to Pittsburgh and in Logstown, some eighteen miles down the Ohio. The plans did not include a fort in Pittsburgh (spelled "Pittsburg" off and on until 1911) at that time.

The original goal of the French was to establish a fort at Barcelona, New York, at the mouth of a creek that flowed into Lake Erie. From there, they believed that it might provide an easy portage on Chatakoin Lake—today known as Chautauqua Lake—where they thought a water route to the interior existed using the Conewango Creek to get to the Allegheny River. This expedition was being managed by Pean, who, upon arrival, started construction of the fort.

Within a few weeks, Marin arrived at the site, and immediately, a heated debate ensued on the total unsuitability of the Barcelona site for their purposes. Marin believed that the Barcelona approach would be perilous, especially for the weighed-down freight canoes that the French intended to have travel over the portage to Chatakoin Lake. He believed that they could not be dragged up on shore like a much smaller bark canoe when the wind and waves of Lake Erie were beating high on a shore bordered with many sandbars, rocks and reefs. The shore provided no shelter whatsoever.

After only three days, Marin ordered Le Mercier to go west along the shore and look for a better location for a fort and storage area. In addition, he was asked to find whether there might also be a convenient route south from that location. Marin only had an old map that had been hand drawn by a French voyageur many years before. It showed a sheltered area marked with an *H* for harbor just thirteen leagues to the west of Barcelona. This new information marks the first historical mention of Presque Isle Bay in official records.

No one was sure regarding the mood and nature of the Indians they might meet. Marin also realized that the Indians would most likely resist the French movement into their territories. After just three days, Le Mercier was back to tell Marin of a natural harbor he had discovered just a short distance away. He also reported that the Indians disclosed a water route south that only required a short portage to a sizeable creek flowing to a great river. Duquesne himself later called this harbor at Erie "the finest spot in nature." It took no time at all to decide to build the fort at Presqu'ile (meaning "almost island" in French).

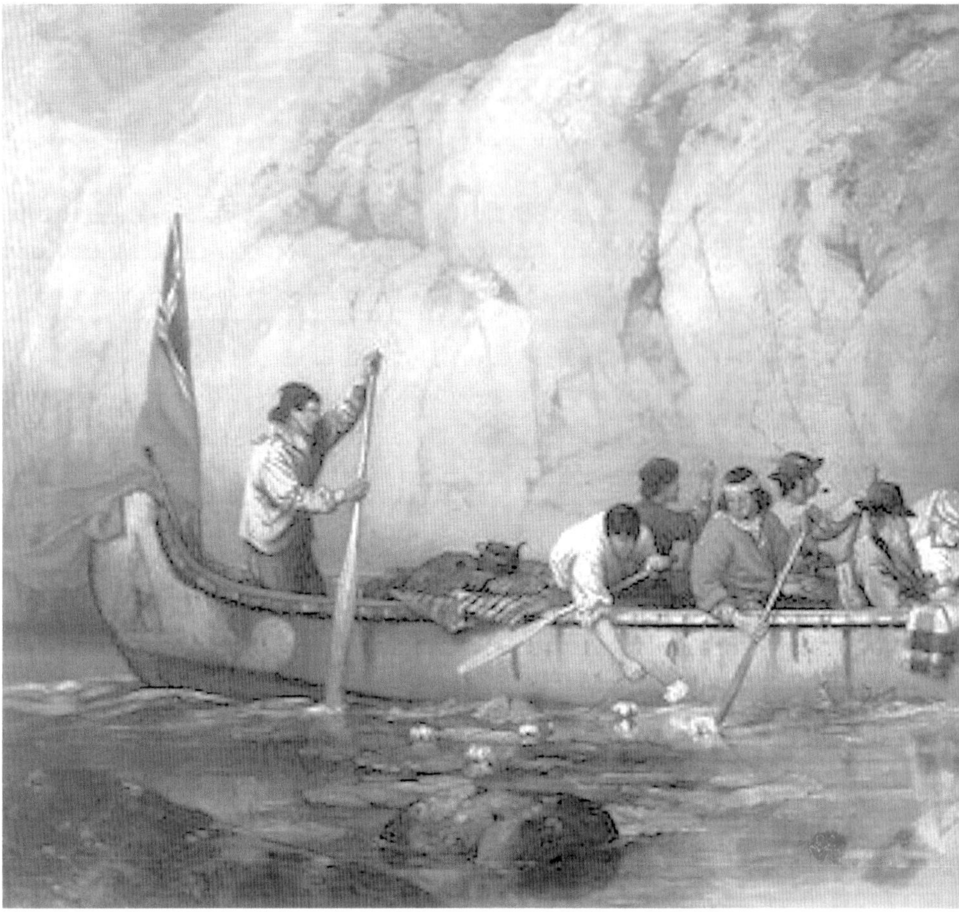

The earliest visitors to Presqu'ile, who arrived on May 3, 1753, soon recognized the potential of the sheltered natural harbor. All of the experienced mariners expressed that, with time, Presque Isle (the English spelling) would become a major trading port on the Great Lakes. The French soldiers of the garrison set to building the fort immediately and located it on a small hill and cliff near the harbor entrance. As with all French forts, this was a strictly military operation. The French did not support or encourage any settlers to live close to the forts, even though a small group of settlers did develop the land just outside the fort.

While today no one knows the exact location of the French fort, most believe it was just west of where the Soldiers and Sailors Home is located today. Most reports show that the front of the fort where the main gate was located sat nearly three hundred yards back from the lake, and a rear gate

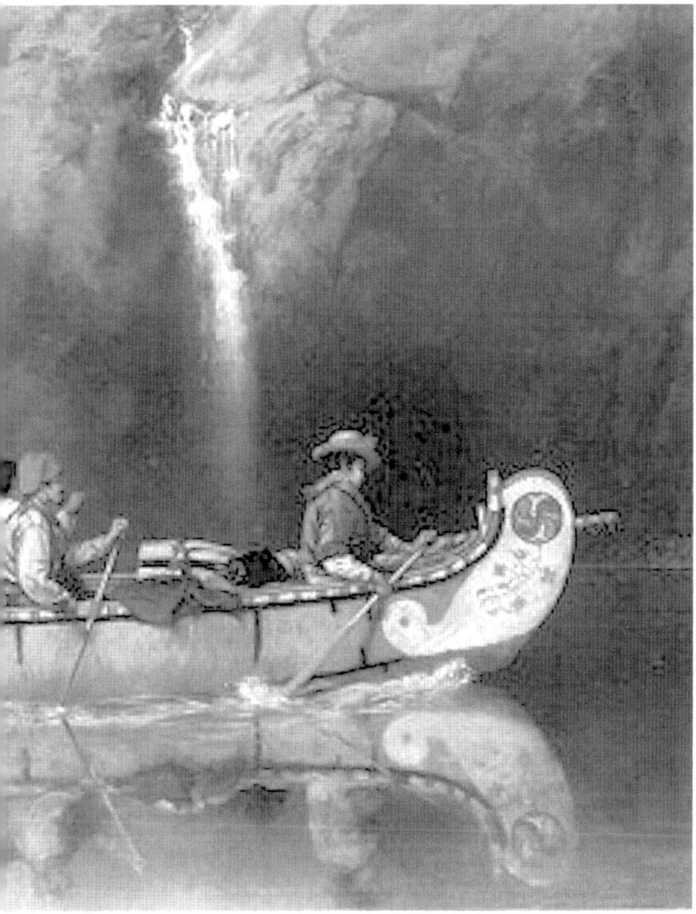

A drawing of an Indian freight canoe used by early French explorers to travel the Great Lakes. *From Wikimedia Commons.*

faced out on an under-construction crude road to Le Boeuf. Marin's plan had been to transform an old Indian path from Presqu'ile to LeBoeuf Creek into a major military road. It was to include bridges across all streams and possibly a storehouse with a horse barn at the halfway point.

By January 10, 1754, the fort—now garrisoned with one hundred men—was busy putting finishing touches on the outer structures and the fort itself. In his orders to build on this site, Governor Duquesne said:

> *In addition to the safety that a post will give us, it is the place, so I have been assured there is the best hunting, fishing, fertile land, and immense meadows to feed and raise cattle, where Indian corn grows with unequaled abundance so that it need only to be sown.*

By August 3, the garrison commander, Sieur de Marin, reported back to the governor that the fort at Presqu'ile was completed. Built from local chestnut logs cut to square, it was installed to a height of fifteen feet. He also reported that the road mentioned previously would be made of hardwood planks, rough-cut logs, mud and stone. This road led to the site where a second fort would be built. The area later became Waterford. The French called the area LeBoeuf after the many buffalos that grazed south of the area.

Marin told Duquesne that this smaller fort with two strategic storage buildings needed to be built in the area near a large creek leading south. Today, that waterway is known as French Creek. Historical records show the road that he finally built was more of a path than a real road. For the most part, it was narrow and just four feet wide. In fact, it was just a cleared trail that a man and a single horse could traverse carrying a pack of no more than four hundred pounds. Because the road was rough, bumpy and wet, a large storage building was going to be needed at the midway point. It would be used to store provisions and supplies for further transport when wagons became bogged down in wet weather.

On July 12, 1754, Marin's brigade began the construction of Fort LeBoeuf. By September, the French had already begun to transport all their supplies over the Niagara Portage and then by large canoes to Presqu'ile. From there, they were hoping to move most of the material and supplies to LeBoeuf. They then planned to move down French Creek and the Allegheny River, southward to Pittsburgh. At one point, a fleet of 120 freight canoes led by Pean had made the voyage to Presqu'ile in a single week. But that year, the French could go no farther than Fort LeBoeuf. A long dry spell made all streams in the area too shallow to float their canoes. While they waited, a serious disease broke out among the troops, causing still more problems for the French explorers. Besides these problems, some of the local Indians became more hostile to the French intrusions into their areas.

The almost daily water traffic in and out of Presqu'ile firmly established the value of its sheltered harbor and large bay. It did not take long for the word to spread that the French fort at Presqu'ile was open and was a good stopping-off point. Almost immediately, many ships were drawn to the new harbor. This was the beginning of the town and port of Presque Isle/Erie. However, the French military powers that had brought with them the mandatory priests who always traveled with their expeditions began enforcing the strict rule that only Catholics were permitted within the walls of the fort. That rule, which was enforced at all French forts in the New World, angered Catholics and non-Catholics alike. It was one factor that would eventually contribute to the ultimate banishment of the French from most of colonial North America.

Right from the beginning of their founding of these forts, the French were under much apprehension as to the movements and strength of British forces in the area west of the Appalachian Mountains. They had no trust at all in Britain's purposes in the area. The French were constantly hearing rumors about the British intentions to remove them from this area and take all their forts, plus any villages nearby. The French were able to maintain the forts in this area until 1759, when the increasing pressure of advancing British troops forced them to retreat to Detroit. Rather than allow the British to walk in and take the various forts, they burned most of them to the ground before they retreated.

Soon after the British had successfully driven the French from this area, they began to rebuild the fort on Presque Isle in the same general area as the old French fort. Late in 1760, British major Robert Rodger arrived in the area to take official possession and control of all forts on Lake Erie and inland for the English. This immediately caused problems with the local Indians of the area. They did not like the English taking control of the region. This was due to what the Indians called bad blood between their people and the British. The main and most vocal dissenter among the Indian communities was a prophet leader and the chief of the Ottawa tribe named Pontiac. He preached far and wide about the friendliness of the French and the selfish total greed of the English. Most of the Indians of the region heard him and followed him willingly and enthusiastically. Pontiac, a masterful speaker and leader, assembled an enormous coalition of tribes, including the Six Nations of the Iroquois, to oppose the British.

In one sweeping, quick, rancorous and bloody group of attacks, Pontiac and his united tribes struck all the British forts throughout the Great Lakes and the Ohio Valley. In early June, they took both Fort Presque Isle and Fort LeBoeuf. In less than one week, the whole area reverted to Indian control. Eventually, the British quelled the uprisings and retook most of the forts, but now troubles with greedy colonists on the eastern seaboard worked to keep British attention away from any development on the Great Lakes, including Presque Isle.

Unfortunately, the official treaty with the French was constantly delayed and was not signed in Paris until 1763. All this happened after the problems with Pontiac were solved by General "Mad" Anthony Wayne. In spite of this treaty with the French, trouble was still to haunt the Great Lakes and other western settlement areas. This was because Lord George Grenville, at the command of King George III, wanted little or nothing to do with any further problems with the North American Indians. On specific order of the king, on October 3, 1763, he issued a royal proclamation that forbade all settlers from living past a line drawn along the Appalachian Mountains. Its actual geographic location is similar to the Eastern Continental Divide's path, running northward from Georgia to the Pennsylvania–New York State border and northeastward past the drainage divide on the St. Lawrence and from there northward through New England.

The proclamation was an effort to appease the Native Americans, and it barred colonial settlement west of the Allegheny Mountains in Pennsylvania. It went one step further and ordered that all colonists already settled in the region remove themselves. If totally followed, this would have negated colonists' claims to the property they had purchased, were already living on and where they had built farms and homes many years prior to the order. This proclamation halted any further westward colonial expansion, and it outlawed existing towns and villages.

At the same time, the proclamation began to enforce impossible recent navigation acts passed by the English assemblies. These rules were to be enforced in all the waters of the Atlantic seashore, as well as all inland waters. These new rules levied additional and abusive taxes on the settlers. The British immediately began to enforce these rules and taxes with vigor. The British claim was that the costs to the United Kingdom of the French and Indian War were enormous and the complete fault of the American colonists. The king felt that the colonists had a duty and should be prepared to pay those expenses. Angry colonists chafed under these offensive, rigid controls and high taxes. This hastened the beginning of the end of British rule of the American colonies.

For nearly twenty years following the French and Indian War, Presque Isle languished, and nothing happened in the area. It sat out for almost all of the American Revolution due to the effects of continuing Indian problems, the total noninterest from East Coast politicians and the lingering effects of King George's various proclamations.

In 1792, the Commonwealth of Pennsylvania wisely arranged for the purchase of the Erie Triangle from the federal government, and slowly, progress started. Ultimately, in 1795, the commonwealth's legislature passed an act establishing a town at Presque Isle and officially named it Erie. Subsequently, the legislature hired Andrew Ellicott and General William

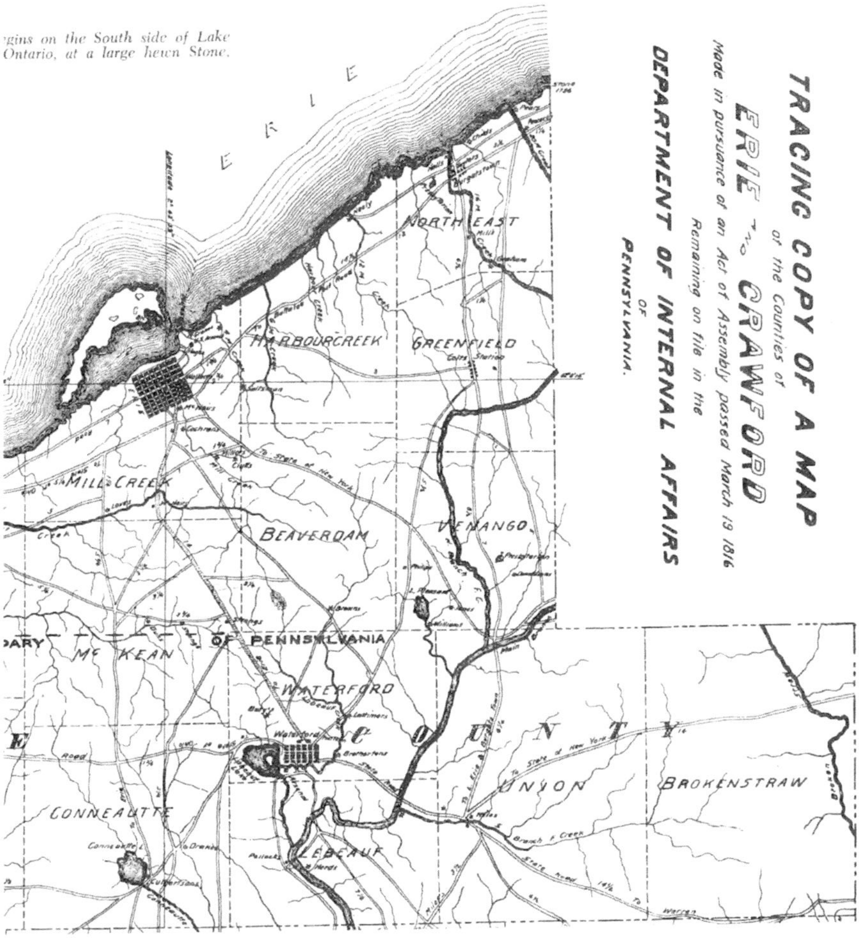

A drawing of early Erie, 1816. *Courtesy of the Erie County Historical Society.*

Irvine to survey and lay out the town and harbor of Erie, along with the towns of Warren, Franklin and Waterford.

Soon Erie enjoyed commercial importance, owing to the recognition of its excellent natural harbor and the deep water of Presque Isle Bay, which was four and a half miles long and an average of one and a half miles wide. The area around Erie was truly unlike any other port on the Great Lakes. In general, the Great Lakes are characterized by steep and eroding shale cliffs, which offer few, if any, natural ports. Another factor in the success of the port of Erie was that the fairly level harbor shores of Presque Isle Bay provided a nearly continuous easy-access shoreline for the building of docks, piers and warehouses. The fact that three major creeks were flowing into the bay also played a major part in the growth of Erie as a successful port city. For these reasons, almost immediately, salt from the Syracuse, New York area became the first and foremost merchandise of a prosperous, waterborne business as it began funneling through the harbor and southward down French Creek and the Allegheny River.

As might have been expected with the sheltered natural harbor with three significant streams entering it—and with three major streams to the west of Presque Isle and four to the east—Erie quickly began to develop as a major shipbuilding and fishing haven. The first known American sailing vessel built on Lake Erie was the *Washington*, which was launched just east of the harbor at Four Mile Creek late in 1797. For many years, there was some conjecture that it might have been launched at Sixteen Mile Creek. However, most documents seem to indicate that Four Mile Creek was the actual location.

As the War of 1812 loomed, Daniel Dobbins, shipbuilder and master of two of the vessels launched from Erie in the early years, in partnership with Rufus Reed, approached military authorities in Washington with a proposal to build a six-gunboat fleet at the Erie harbor to challenge the British fleet patrolling on Lake Erie. Of course, this historical adventure is a long story in and of itself and has been the subject of many books. Dobbins's idea turned out to be a key factor in the United States finally gaining its full freedom from the British, as the Battle of Lake Erie became the first victory and full capture of an entire British sailing fleet. It was the singular event that put Erie in the national spotlight and helped shape its future as a major Great Lakes port city. Since that time, the twin industries of shipbuilding and commercial shipping have proven to be two of the most stable and active industries in the city and harbor.

After the War of 1812, the very advantage that Dobbins had used in his pitch about the Erie harbor—the large, protecting sandbars across the harbor entrance—became a problem in the expansion of trade through the port. An example of this is that *Walk-on-the-Water*, the first steamship on Lake Erie, could not enter the harbor

Sailing vessels built and launched in Erie harbor's early years were:

The Good Intent
Harlequin
Mary
Wilkinson
Washington

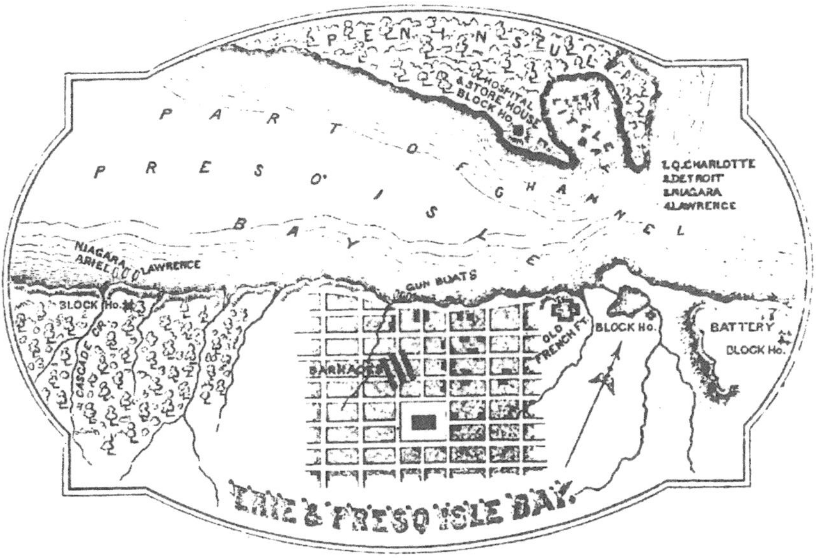

Erie harbor as it was at the start of the War of 1812. *Courtesy of the Pennsylvania DCNR files.*

to load and unload cargo. It had to do so at Four Mile or Twelve Mile Creek instead. As a result of these limitations, plans were made through federal and state cooperation to dredge, straighten and deepen the harbor entrance. After this work was completed, the Erie harbor moved into a period of rapid growth. Erie native Rufus Reed became the most prominent sailboat and steamship owner in the area.

Reed constructed a series of docks on the bay front, with the largest being at the foot of Sassafras Street. During this period, a new industry that lives on even today was born in the harbor. Erie became a natural place for vessels to spend the winter season in the sheltered Erie harbor and have necessary repairs or improvements made while there.

The next major development to reach Erie and expand the use of its port was the Erie Extension Canal. In 1839, work began on a canal that would connect Erie to Pittsburgh, with its steel industry and associated coal fields. The canal was completed in 1844. Rufus Reed became its primary shareholder. The canal, which followed part of Lee's Run Creek's original path, entered Presque Isle Bay right above Reed's Sassafras dock area, making Erie's harbor an important source of the Pennsylvania coal that was shipped west on the Great Lakes. Conversely, canalboats returning to Pittsburgh

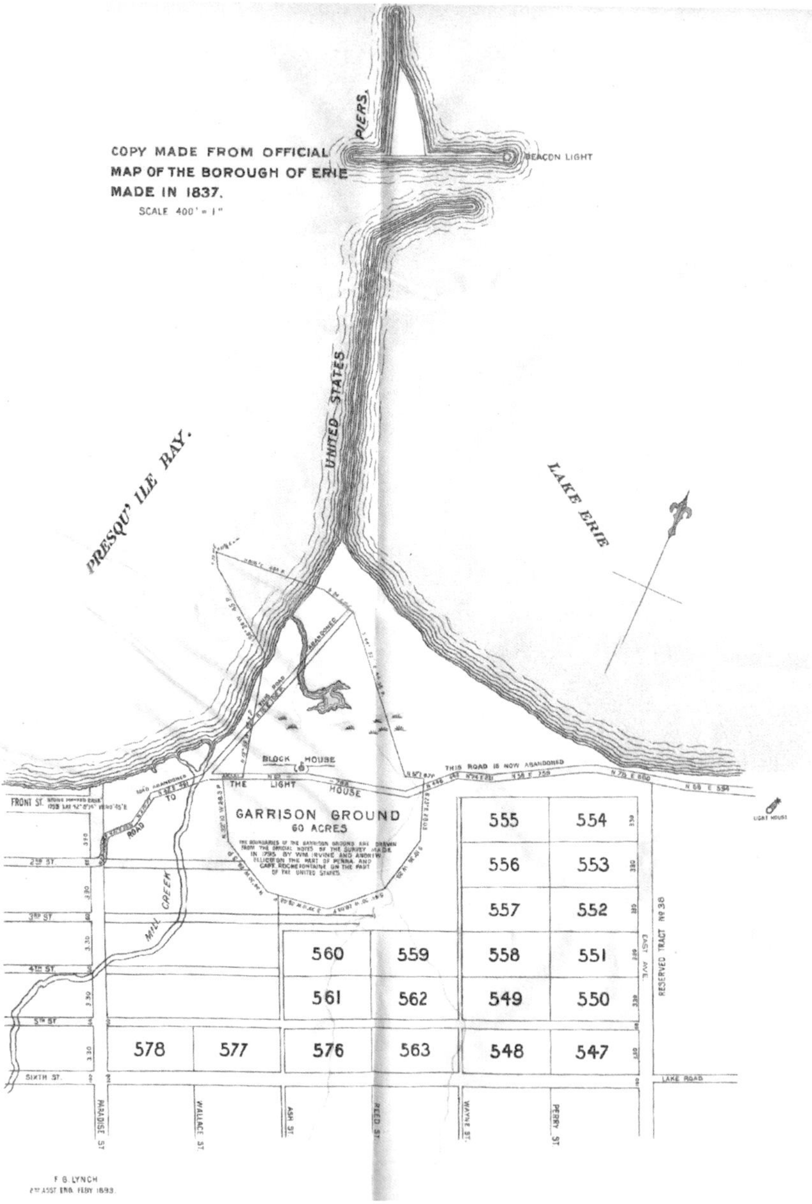

An 1890 drawing of Erie harbor. *Courtesy of the Pennsylvania DCNR files.*

were usually loaded with iron ore from the mines near Lake Michigan and also with assorted freight. This route also became quite popular with the settlers seeking to head farther west through Pittsburgh and down the Ohio River to the western territories.

Interestingly, a whole new industry started on Erie's waterfront thanks to this new route west for the settlers. Many families soon found that they needed slightly smaller barge-like boats to go farther down the Ohio River into western areas. It did not take long for the shippers to discover that by building and using smaller barges, they could make extra money selling these boats to the pioneers after arrival in Pittsburgh. These boats would be built in Erie and go down to Pittsburgh loaded with people and goods, where the families would buy the boats and reload them to continue their trips west. Some boaters also used the canal to travel to and from Erie for pleasure. The three-day trip soon became long party weekends for some. During the period, traffic within the harbor increased tenfold.

An interesting fact found in long-forgotten government statistics from 1869 was a report that detailed that the total marine commerce on the Great Lakes exceeded the whole Atlantic coastal trade of the United States. This may seem a bit strange until one realizes that, in order to move goods throughout the Midwest and to interior cities, the Great Lakes acted like a superhighway.

The fact is that before 1860, there were just a few established railroads. There were none to the harbor back then, and there were even fewer reliable and passable roads to service the port and areas inland. So until roads and railroads could be built and become consistently dependable, water travel was the only way to move goods and people safely, quickly and at an affordable cost. Erie's harbor, with its long-established and natural connection through Waterford and down French Creek to the Allegheny River, provided a cheap and logical way to get goods and people to Pittsburgh and points west on the Ohio River. In 1844, when the Erie Extension Canal opened for business in the Erie harbor, it started a new boom for the port.

With the colossal increase in ships moving in and out of the harbor, there came a real need to provide them with some form of navigation aids. That now brings us to the rest of this book, which is devoted to the story of the three lighthouses standing as sentinels protecting mariners on Lake Erie since the opening of the original Presque Isle Light in 1819.

2

WHY THREE LIGHTHOUSES AT ERIE?

In researching this book, I learned more and more about lighthouses, like where they are usually located and why they are placed there. Erie, being centrally located on Lake Erie, is both lucky and unlucky for its location. Lake Erie sometimes causes unique weather and lake structures off its shores that affect daily life. Ever since people have traveled the Great Lakes, storms have ravaged their trips and taken lives and vessels. Many people have told me about their trips down the lake from the Buffalo area, where they would leave on a clear day and be forced to put into the Erie harbor just a few hours later to evade a vicious storm or huge fog bank. The lake is known for its unpredictable gales, blizzards, fog banks and thunderstorms that can overwhelm the lake without warning. These are often caused by polar-chilled fronts from Canada's north smashing together with the saturated warm winds from the southern United States.

The first sailing ship on the upper Great Lakes, *Le Griffon*, set out from the Niagara River area at Cayuga Creek. It made a successful voyage to Green Bay but totally disappeared on its return trip, never to be heard from again. One very scary figure about the dangers of the Great Lakes is that in the twenty-year period from 1878 to 1898, nearly six thousand vessels were wrecked on the Great Lakes, and two thousand of those were not salvageable.

Over the years, it has been found that any large expanse of water that allows waves to build to substantial heights, paired with tempestuous weather conditions, can also produce dense fog, lake-effect storms and wildly fluctuating water levels. The shallowest of the Great Lakes and the only one on a near-perfect northeast–southwest axis is Lake Erie. It produces some of the world's most infamous weather patterns. They range from lake-effect snow to irrational storm surges that can lower lake levels eight to ten feet on one side of the lake while raising them twice as high in certain areas across the lake. All of this can cause innumerable problems for the ships and other vessels.

> *Lake Erie holds the record for being the shallowest of the five Great Lakes and consequently has a history of kicking up a fuss in the least time. A breath of wind is enough to make her do somersaults and turn handsprings.*
> —*William Ratigan,* Great Lakes Shipwrecks and Survivals

In a series of Great Lakes storms in 1868 and 1869, a total of thirty-seven ships were lost. These losses were one of the main reasons for the establishment of a national weather forecasting service. In the beginning, it was operated by the U.S. Army Signal Corps using telegraphs to announce approaching storms in a few major port cities. In its earliest days, it was also able to warn of possible seiches. These are short-term, irregular lake level changes. They are known worldwide but are not very common. They are simply a standing wave of large, yet not necessarily seen, proportions forming within an enclosed body of water. Today, and back as far as the early 1900s, they were called rogue waves. Small, rhythmic seiches are always present in large lakes. On the Great Lakes, and Lakes Erie and Ontario in particular, they are always present. In the past, some have taken lives, swept people from beaches and destroyed boats, piers and homes along the shorelines. The problem is that, due to their very nature, they are usually imperceptible to the naked eye. This sounds strange but is true.

This, plus the fact that Lake Erie is particularly subject to many unusual wind-caused aberrations due to its length, shallowness and its elongation on the northeast-southwest axis, can cause enormous problems for sailing vessels. Now, if you add the fact that the prevailing winds on the lake nearly match this precise direction, you have a formula for potential disaster.

To provide the perfect storm for tragedies, Lake Erie also has what many call the "Lake Erie Quadrangle." This is an area that runs across the lake almost exactly where Long Point, Canada, sits across the lake from Presque Isle State Park. The border of this large area of central Lake Erie begins on the western side at Conneaut, Ohio, and then moves straight across the lake to Port Burwell, Ontario. On the eastern side, an almost parallel

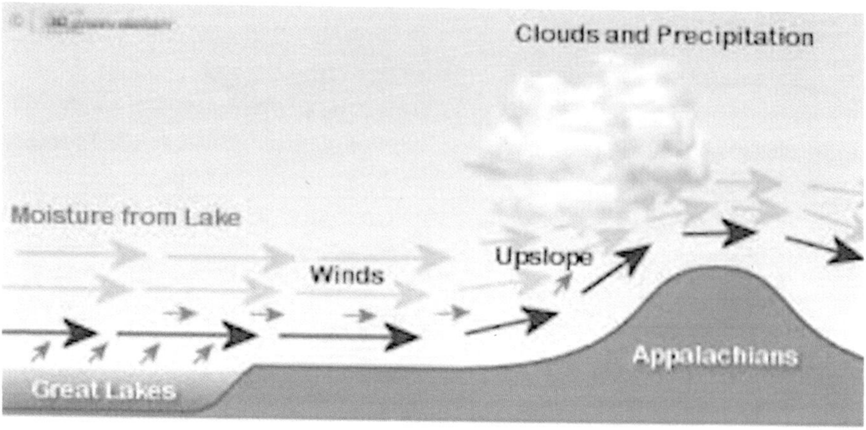

A drawing showing how lake-effect clouds and precipitation happens in Lake Erie. *Courtesy of the National Weather Service, Washington, D.C.*

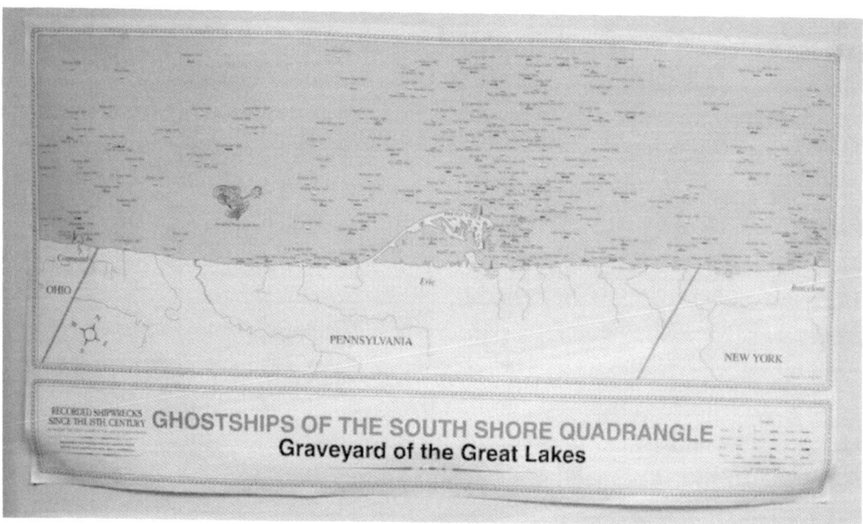

The Lake Erie Quadrangle, also known as the Graveyard of the Great Lakes. *Courtesy of the Erie County Historical Society and the Pennsylvania DCNR files.*

line can be plotted from Barcelona, New York, to Peacock Point, Ontario. The area contained within these lines has become known as the Lake Erie Quadrangle. It is truly the graveyard of the Great Lakes and an area where more vessels are lost than most areas of the world (see map above).

Why do so many wrecks occur here? The answers are varied, but the main reason certainly centers on Lake Erie's total unpredictability. One minute, it is as gentle as a kitten, and in just minutes, it can turn into a wild boar. Yet there are other factors that must be added into any explanation of the number of deaths and wrecks that appear to happen in this rather small section of the Great Lakes. I have heard of nearly twenty factors that may cause this, but I believe most can be attributed to just ten major factors, which are:

- the volume of traffic on the lake
- unreliability of many vessels regarding safety and maintenance
- crossing and turning patterns getting into sheltered harbors like the Erie and Long Point communities
- fog and major freak storms that tend to develop quickly
- poor weather forecasting teamed with irregular storms
- unnecessarily running for shore before an approaching storm
- geography of the area—two major sand spits with rather shallow waters nearby
- few lighthouses or light buoys
- few sheltered harbors available
- poor boatmanship skills

All that is necessary to understand why Erie has the privilege of having three lighthouses is to look carefully at the map on the previous page. This map is only two-thirds of the area of the Lake Erie Quadrangle, and each name or mark on that map denotes a wreck or sunken vessel. This area is truly a graveyard of ships. One additional fact you need to consider is that it *does not* include any modern-day pleasure crafts, which would most likely double the marks on the map.

3

THE ORIGINAL PRESQUE ISLE LIGHT

"Monument to Bygone Years"

Children playing at its base,
Never glance her way.
Artists keep daily vigils to capture her beauty.
Old and faithful,
She stands as a lonely sentinel.
Her ever-searching beams light your way.

Weathered by time, wind and sun.
Yet,
Still strong, unyielding and proud.
She sits within a rainbow of color and light.
A monument to bygone years.
—Eugene H. Ware

We all know that Lake Erie is certainly not an ocean but a lake. A body of water is only considered a lake if it is surrounded by land and is large enough to have a wave-swept shoreline. The rest are deemed ponds. What most people do not realize is exactly how large Lake Erie really is. The lake, which has over ten thousand square miles of surface area, ranks as the twelfth largest lake in the world. Many a boater on Lake Erie can tell you stories of having to run rapidly to a safe harbor because perfect weather

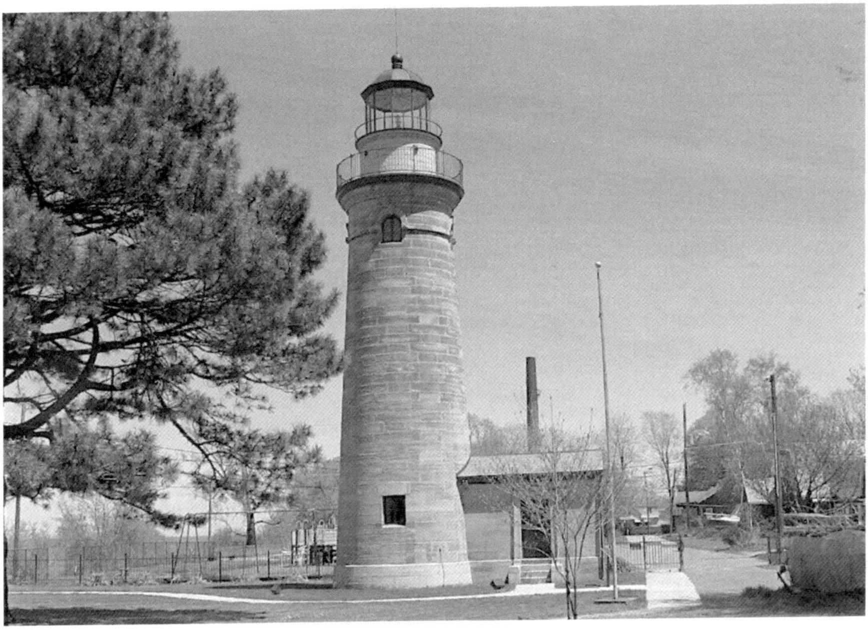

Erie Land Lighthouse, 2006. *Author's collection.*

has turned appalling within a few minutes. Even in calm conditions, Lake Erie has been known to generate six- to eight-foot waves within just fifteen to twenty minutes.

That is why, back in the 1790s, quite a few fishermen and cargo haulers commenced using the sheltered harbor at Erie as their base for the shipping of salt. Salt was then, and is even today, a much sought-after commodity, one used as both a handy preservative and palate-pleasing condiment. Three of Erie's most well-known and prominent citizens—Daniel Dobbins, Rufus Reed and Judah Colt—played major roles in the shipping coming in and out of the Port of Erie. They all had a part in the changes that came to the Erie waterfront.

> *Lighthouses are intriguing because they're a part of a frontier that we haven't conquered yet. The sea is the last frontier on earth.*
>
> —*Elinor De Wire*

By the turn of the century, as mentioned in Chapter 1, Dobbins and Reed had unofficially become working partners in the shipping and boat building businesses in the Port of Erie. Dobbins was exceptionally vocal about the

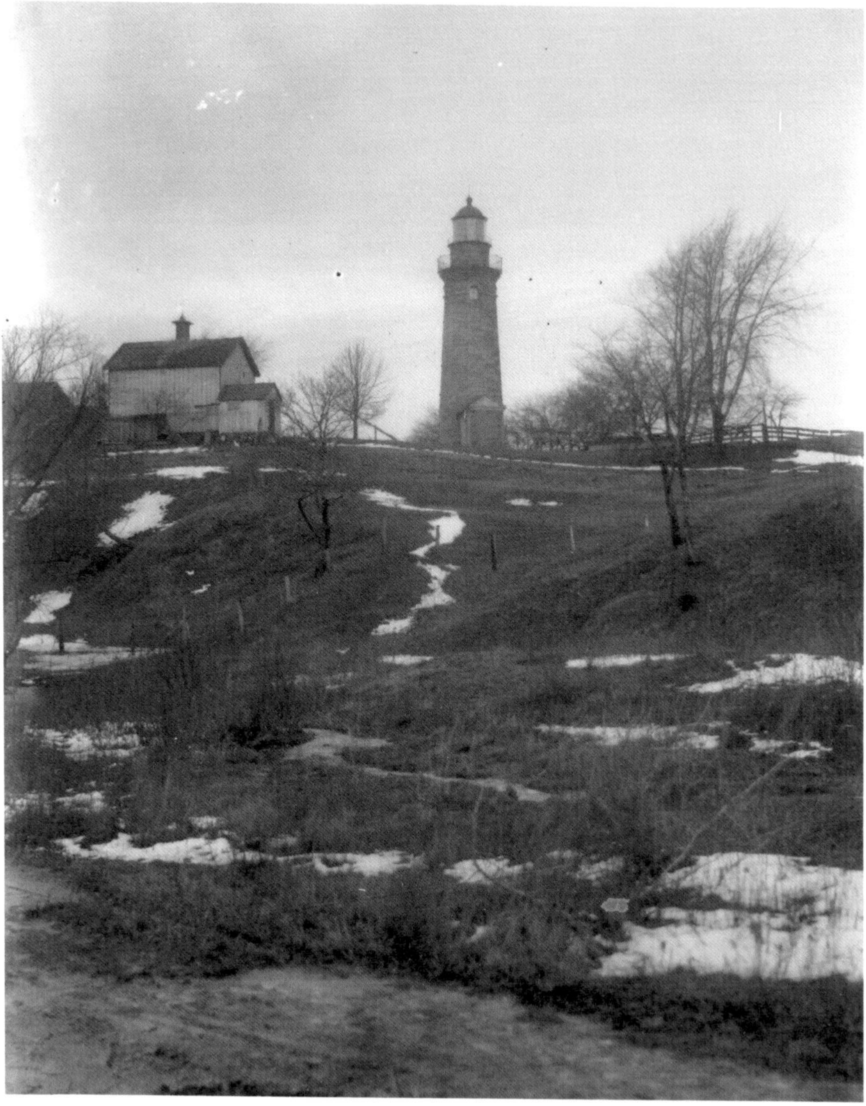

The Land Lighthouse in 1896 with a barn and pasture on the lighthouse grounds. *Courtesy of the Erie County Historical Society.*

current and future usefulness of the harbor and port. He had been quietly campaigning for some form of aid to navigation outside the harbor entrance on the cliffs east of the town for many years. He heard rumors in 1806 from Captain William Lee of Chippewa, New York, near Buffalo, that a lighthouse had been approved for the harbor at Buffalo. On hearing this, he became enraged that Erie did not also get approval. He felt the need in Erie was much greater than in Buffalo. The never shy or withdrawn Dobbins began a letter-writing campaign to the federal government about the establishment of a lighthouse east of Erie. He even expressed a certain joy over the lack of funding for the Buffalo Lighthouse, which was somehow forgotten in the legislation.

Old records show that in 1810, only ten sailing vessels of over fifteen tons, considered large at the time, sailed on Lake Erie. However, a large number of smaller vessels kept the ports on Lake Erie exceedingly busy. Some of the larger ships could not always get into the Erie harbor due to the sandbars, which at low water levels could limit the depth of the navigation channel to only six to eight feet.

Judah Colt—then head of the Population Company in Erie, which was the major land company in the area—was also involved with shipping. He owned a few ships and also worked with other ship owners. Colt did much of his shipping using piers he built at the major streams along the lakeshore. These waterways included Walnut and Elk Creeks on the west side of Erie and Four Mile and Sixteen Mile Creeks on the east side of town. He built two large and substantial piers at the east side locations.

Many vessels owned by other shippers were permitted to use Colt's docks to bring goods to Erie. He usually purchased goods from these shippers. Colt, a shrewd businessman, used his shipping ventures to gain control of nearly 100 percent of the general trade of the area. He owned and ran three general stores at various locations within the community, and all other stores and businesses were coerced to buy from him since he controlled the import of nearly all needed goods to the area. If you needed a nail for building or wheat for bread, you would have to buy from a Judah Colt store or at a store he supplied.

During this same time, Rufus Reed was fast becoming a guiding force in the small community. In 1810, Erie had only about four hundred permanent residents. In fact, Rufus's father, Seth Reed, had previously started Erie's first business enterprise. His father built the first home in Erie near Second and Parade Streets. Within six months, he started using it as a public house, providing room, food and drinks to clients. He called it the Presque Isle Hotel and, without delay, nailed a sign on the front of his home. A larger hotel just two blocks away from his household, which his sons operated for him, quickly followed this.

Rufus quickly became immersed in the family business and soon expanded into many other ventures. He owned and operated a sawmill, a shipyard, a construction company, two gristmills and a distillery. As mentioned in Chapter 1, one of his most recognized accomplishments was the building of large docks and warehouses at the foot of the Erie Extension Canal on the bay front, once it was opened. This was his most successful endeavor and helped Erie grow at a rapid rate. His many partnerships and close work with Daniel Dobbins guaranteed the success of many of his businesses and of his growing influence throughout the area.

During this time, Daniel Dobbins continued to put pressure on the government in Washington to build a lighthouse at Presque Isle, and he had solid support from the Commonwealth of Pennsylvania for this effort. It finally paid off. In 1810, Congress did authorize the building of two lighthouses on Lake Erie. The reauthorization of the Buffalo Lighthouse was approved, but this time, it included the actual funding for the project. Congress also authorized the building and funding of a lighthouse east of what was to become the town of Erie on a high cliff overlooking the lake. At the time of this authorization, Erie was known as the town of Presque

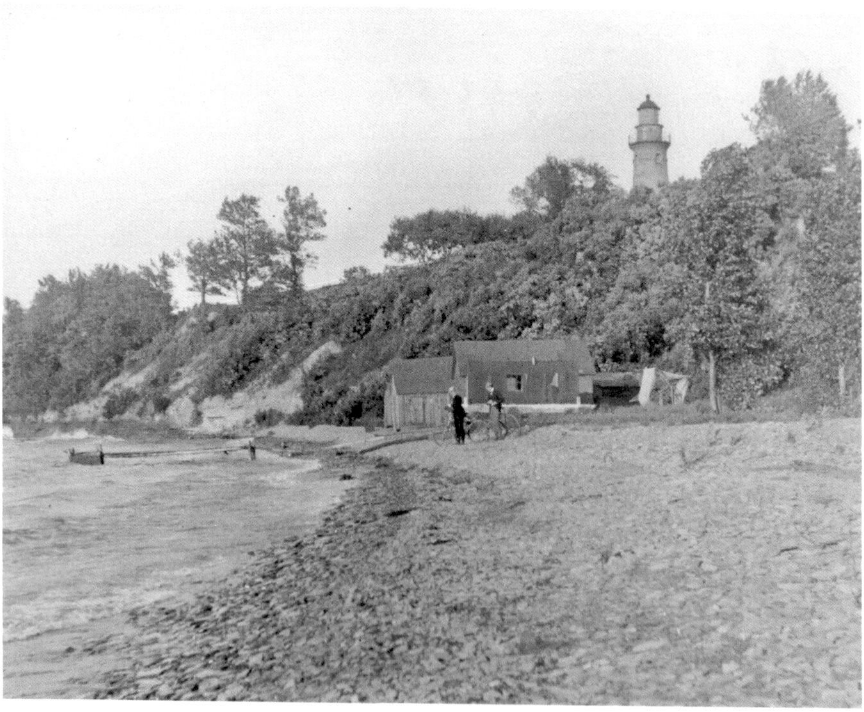

A view of the Land Lighthouse from the beach in 1890, showing a wooden fishing pier and two men on bicycles. *Courtesy of the Erie County Historical Society.*

Isle. Shortly after this, a local citizen, Brigadier General John Kelso of the Pennsylvania Militia, donated a minimum of two acres and up to four acres of land if needed for the lighthouse. This seemed like a blessing at the time but, over the years, turned into an unintentional disaster.

KEY FACTS ABOUT THE ERIE LAND LIGHTHOUSE

BUILT	1818	original lighthouse	twenty-foot tower
	1857	second lighthouse	fifty-six-foot tower
	1867	present lighthouse	forty-nine-foot tower
STYLE	conical sandstone with brick lining*		
TOWER	forty-nine feet tall sixty-nine steps to lantern room		
LENS	third-order Fresnel lens removed in 1901 and moved to Marblehead Lighthouse		
LOCATION	Lighthouse Street, Erie, Pennsylvania		
ACCESS	open to the public for scheduled tours picnic and playground facilities on grounds		

* Most information from the early 1800s indicates that the tower was round. No drawings or photographs of the original lighthouse seem to exist. In researching for this book, I was able to find contractor drawings of the planned lighthouse in the National Archives. They indicate that a rectangular tower, not a round tower, was planned.

When the lighthouse was opened in 1818, the mouth of Presque Isle Bay was nearly a mile wide and was obstructed by a series of three sandbars. When the water was low, the channel offered only six to eight feet of water on which ships could navigate. Even with a lighthouse now in place on the cliffs outside the harbor, the final navigation of the channel was still difficult as a result of the shifting sands caused by storms and currents. These ever-changing sands perpetually altered the depth and location of the main channel into the harbor. This fact further complicated the procedure for ships trying to enter Presque Isle Bay. Many times, ships were forced to anchor outside the harbor and offload cargo onto smaller crafts for final transit into Erie. This caused difficulties and was costly for shippers. Part of the channel problem was that back in those days, few realized that Presque Isle itself was constantly moving eastward and changing in size and location each year.

Shortly after the end of the War of 1812, officials in Washington asked Commodore Perry his opinion on the viability of removing the sandbars. In his answer to Washington, he said they should be removed as soon as feasible. Once the lighthouse was finally operational, the federal government undertook a nine-month survey to study the problem. When the survey was completed, nothing happened.

In 1822, the Commonwealth of Pennsylvania began its own survey of Presque Isle Bay and the channel area. Its goal was to solve the sandbar problem even if the federal government would not. It was at that point that the federal government decided to come back into the picture. It did not take long this time. A project for improving the harbor was undertaken in 1823 and continued through 1827.

After some preliminary work in the lake itself and minor dredging to deepen sections of Presque Isle Bay, the federal government cut through the sandbars and built two parallel piers that were 350 feet apart, forming an entrance from the lake to the bay. The channel was dredged to a uniform 16-foot depth.

When the original Presque Isle Light was built in 1818, the contract called for a twenty-foot-high square tower with an enclosed lantern room sheltering an array of nine separate interchangeable lamps and reflectors. Originally, heavy whale oil fueled the light generated by the fires from the apparatus.

This arrangement of many interchangeable lamps allowed the fueling of the lights to be much easier for the lighthouse keeper because each lamp had its own independent fuel supply. Potentially, one month or more of a supply of fuel could be stored within the light's lantern room, but most of the time, only five fuel containers were filled at a time.

A few historians believe that the Presque Isle Light initially burned kerosene, which was then called refined mineral oil. However, most experts

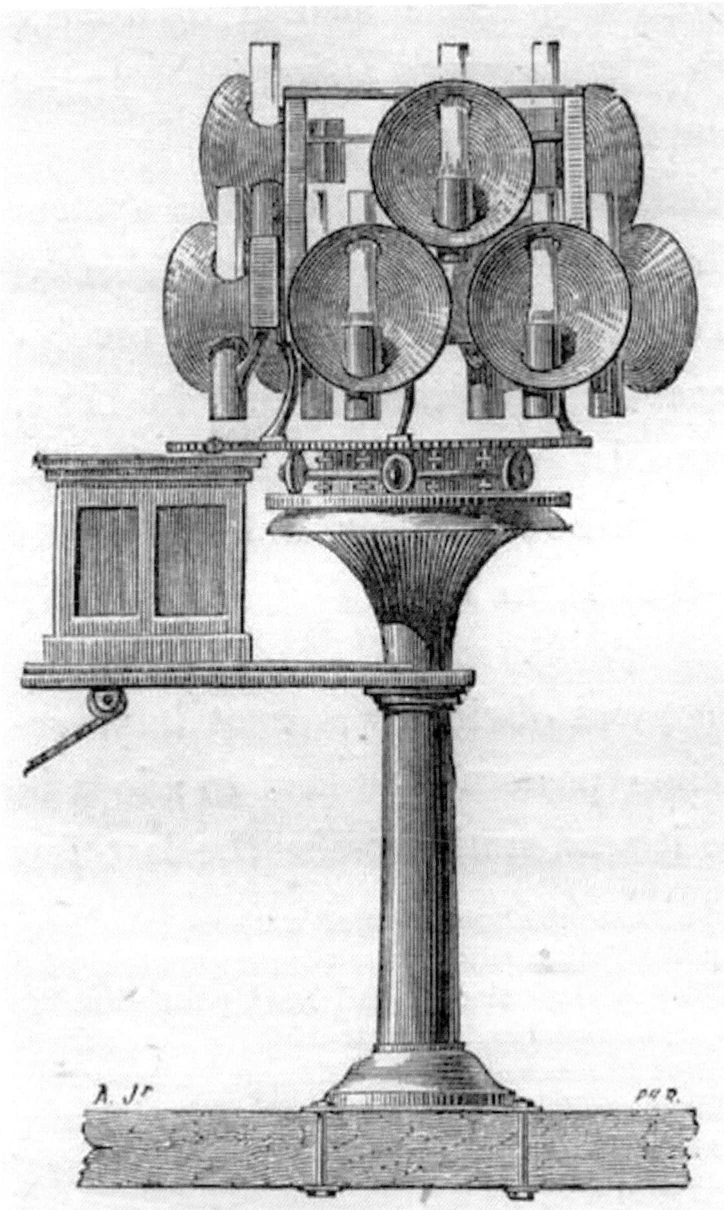

CATOPTRIC APPARATUS.

A lamp array used in the 1800s by many U.S. lighthouses. It was usually fueled by whale oil. *Courtesy of Wikimedia Commons.*

feel that it is very likely that the lighthouse burned sperm whale oil, as did virtually all other lighthouses in the 1818–60 period. There were two grades of whale oil that were used. They were "summer weight," which had a rather thick viscosity, and a "thinner weight," which, in most cases, had to be preheated in colder climates of the United States in the winter months. Many people today believe this use of the majestic whale was disgraceful. But back in the 1800s, whales were plentiful. This oil was used simply because it was the best product available during that period and because it burned fairly clean and bright.

When the price of whale oil increased to the point that the government thought it was getting too high, the fuel was slowly switched to lard oil and, later, to kerosene. Perhaps any real history about this switch to kerosene is made even more interesting due to the fact that it was entirely due to fairly unknown actions during the Civil War. Yes, whale oil became a major victim of this war. The Confederate military had three or more skillful commerce raiders that cruised, with little or no opposition, all along the eastern seacoast. In fact, the Confederate raiders *Shenandoah* and *Alabama* destroyed over forty-six New England whalers. If you take those losses and add them to all the other losses during this period, over 50 percent of all American whalers were sunk.

The notion regarding the Presque Isle Light initially burning kerosene seems to be a mistake of timing and recorded history. When the lighthouse needed to be rebuilt, the final lighthouse did indeed switch and burn kerosene. That, however, was not until after 1867. There was much worry about using the very volatile kerosene in closed areas such as the lantern rooms of lighthouses. It was thought to be too dangerous for lighthouse use, and the few lighthouses that experimented with kerosene recorded many fires and injuries.

Using kerosene became safer and came into common use in Europe when a Swiss physicist, François Pierre Aimé Argand, developed a new type of lamp in which a single air wick was able to safely emit as much light as seven previous lamps. But in the United States, the superintendent of lighthouses, Stephen Pleasonton, would not adopt this lamp because a friend had also developed a very similar lamp. He ordered that only the Lewis lamps be used in all American lighthouses. After ten years of use, it was discovered that this lamp was nothing more than a poorly modified version of the Argand-style lamp. It was also found that the reflectors and other parts of the Lewis lamp were severely flawed. Light keepers soon found that the lamps and the entire assemblies were prone to sooting up and required constant cleaning.

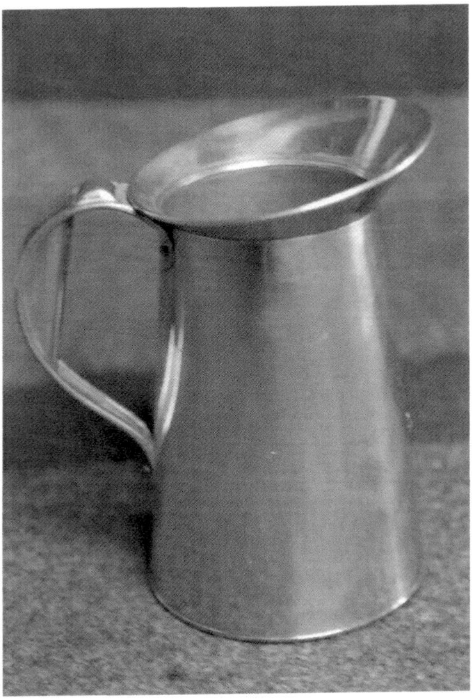

Left: A whale oil container used in 1805. *From* Bruckhaus and Efron Encyclopedic Dictionary, *1890.*

Below: An oil can with a long spout used in the 1800s. *From* Bruckhaus and Efron Encyclopedic Dictionary, *1890.*

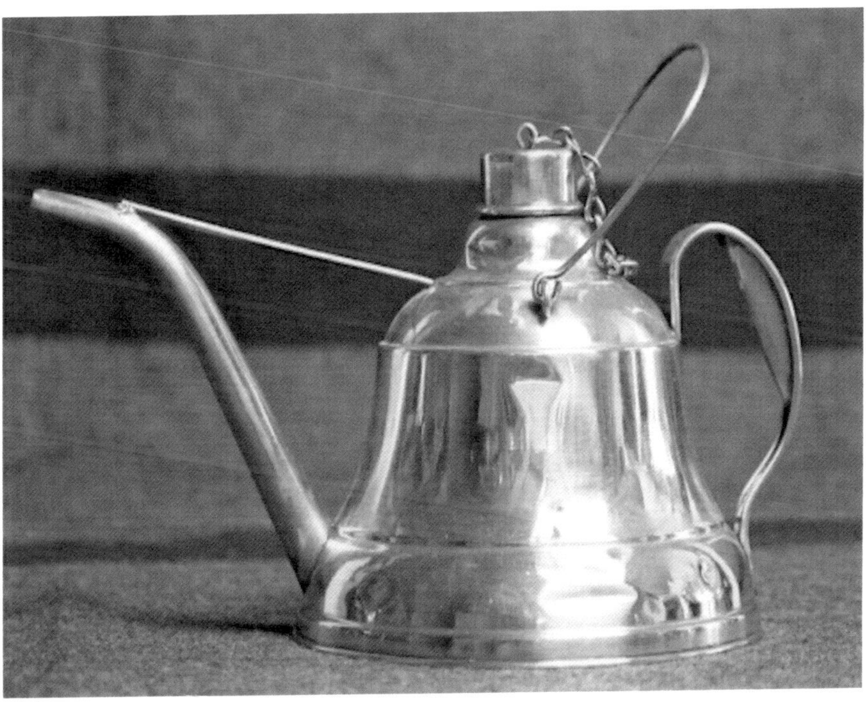

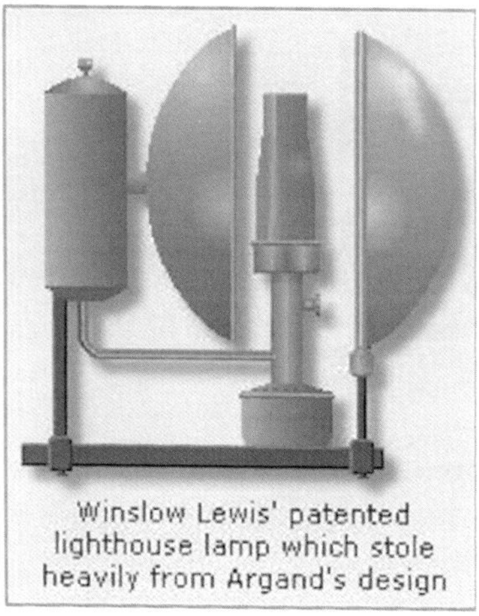

A drawing of a Lewis lamp. *Courtesy of Wikimedia Commons.*

Many historical experts find it extremely interesting that Pleasonton served at the U.S. patent office when Lewis applied for and received his patent approval.

The light sources that were used at the original Presque Isle Light were directed out over the lake by the array of nine lamps and projected by an assembly of lenses, reflectors and prisms that gathered the light and sent it out as a beam. These arrays were part of a light system called catadioptric light systems. Each lighthouse had its array of lamps designed especially for the conditions at that lighthouse.

The original lighthouse had a nine-foot-wide square tower, although many Internet sites still incorrectly state that it was a round tower. Recently, I have been able to find a drawing of this original square tower. The lantern room itself was reached using an iron staircase going directly up to it. The lighthouse was initially built more than two hundred yards west of the current structure and sat over one hundred feet above Lake Erie. Because the lighthouse sat on a nearly eighty-foot-high cliff and was itself twenty feet high, it had a focal height of one hundred feet.This focal height meant that its white beacon could be seen nearly ten miles out in the lake. Once the tower was completed, a one-story brick dwelling with three rooms to accommodate the families of the light keepers was built.

The first keeper of this light was a man in his forties named John Bone, who served from 1818 until 1832. He was a married man with four girls ranging in age from five to over twenty, plus two boys, ages ten and fifteen. This rather large family all moved into the small three-room keeper's house.

During those early years, a lighthouse keeper was held to a pretty strict schedule. In many cases, this led to a lonely life. This took a very special person. The daily routine sometimes was extremely boring, yet at other times, it was exceedingly exciting and difficult. But at all times, it could be counted on to be incredibly demanding. A lighthouse keeper could count on the fact that his job was never going to be a simple nine-to-five occupation. His typical tour of duty began before dusk and continued well past dawn. The lighthouse had to be maintained in a continual state of readiness. There

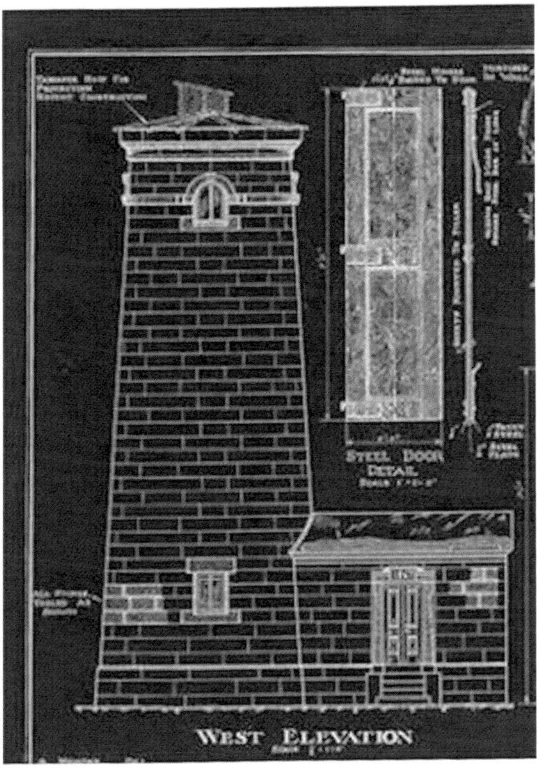

Plans on file in Washington, D.C., for the original Presque Isle Light, now Erie Land Light. *Courtesy of the National Archives, Washington, D.C.*

were routine but essential duties and repairs to be made, and he was always prepared to respond to any emergency, including fires and shipwrecks. One of the keeper's main jobs involved keeping the lenses as clean as possible. If the lenses were dirty, passing ships might not see the light. More keepers were fired for not completing this job properly than for any other reason. However, the keeper's job involved more than keeping the light lit and the lenses clean. It also included tending to the outside windows of the lantern room. That meant working outside in all weather—rain, heat, snow, sleet, strong winds and ice.

During those early days of lighthouse keeping, the government did not supply the families with an allowance for food per person. What that meant was that in addition to "keeping the light," the keeper had to become a farmer to supply his family. Bone himself had two horses and a cow, and there were always twenty to thirty chickens roaming the property. His wife kept a very large garden and even sold some of the extra summer crops to supplement the family income. Hunting and fishing usually became a requirement for early light keepers' families.

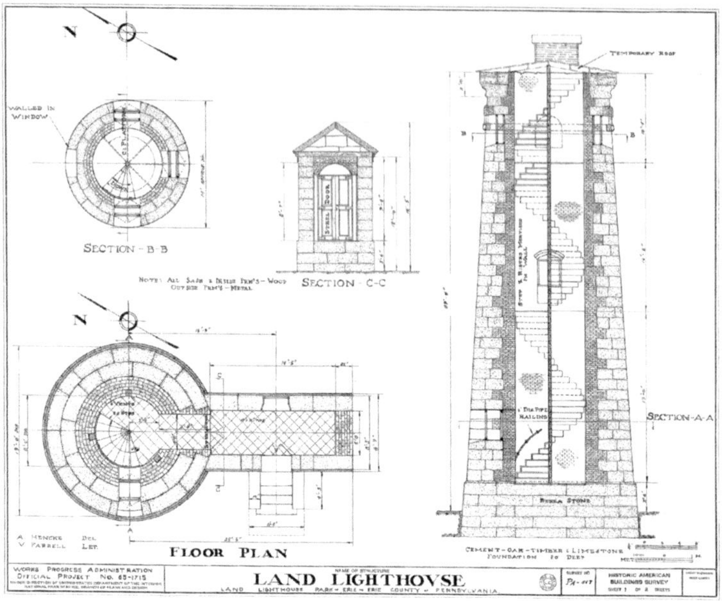

A drawing of the floor plan of the Erie Land Lighthouse obtained through the National Archives. *Courtesy of Jerry Skrypzak.*

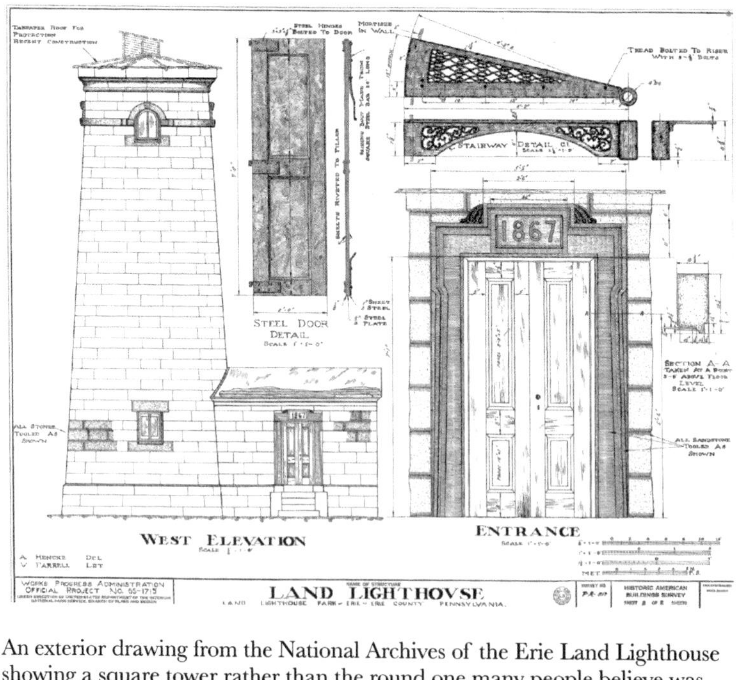

An exterior drawing from the National Archives of the Erie Land Lighthouse showing a square tower rather than the round one many people believe was built. *Courtesy of Jerry Skrypzak.*

It was not until after 1881 that all keepers were required to use a publication called *Instructions to Light-keepers* to accomplish their jobs in what the Lighthouse Service determined was a fitting manner. This rather small book of 124 pages was, and still is, very precise in supplying keepers with information on virtually everything they needed to know about running a lighthouse and explaining it in great and specific detail. Before the Lighthouse Board published this book, any training a keeper received was at best unsystematic and usually careless and haphazard. Historians believe that this lack of training explains why many early lighthouses were in poor and even disastrous condition before the formation of the Lighthouse Board.

Each evening before dark, it was the light keeper's job to enter the oil room, fill the oil cans, check and trim the wicks if necessary and then climb the steps leading to the top of the tower and check which lamps were to be used that night. He would determine which lamps would be used based on which had the best wicks and completely full oil tanks. He would then fill all lamp reservoirs that required additional oil. This was important because most oil reservoirs did not hold enough oil to keep their lamps burning the entire night. The light keeper's very existence was centered on the beacon, which could not be abandoned, even in the most adverse situations. He would then light the lamp, walk out on the viewing platform and stand watch by looking out over the lake to see if any ships were coming in at dusk. Erie was a busy fishing and shipping port, so the keeper's job was very important to the community.

From the very beginning of the Lighthouse Inspection Service, all lighthouses were subject to at least an annual inspection to rate and inspect the building, grounds and quality of service at a particular light station. This inspection was a key factor in safety and service at the original Presque Isle Light. The inspector's job was to make sure that the keepers performed the required work around the lighthouse they served. Keepers sometimes called them the "white glove crews."

Lighthouse work was dirty work, and as pointed out above, cleaning was of paramount importance. Ranking very close to cleaning was keeping the light dressed for visitors. The Lighthouse Service has always encouraged people to visit U.S. lighthouses. With that in mind, the keeper also became a great painter and polisher. At most lighthouses, brass was used throughout, so keeping it looking bright and glistening was continually part of the keeper's job. This meant that cleaning smocks was necessary to keep the required wool uniforms neat and clean. Those smocks were needed so that items like paint, soot and polish could get on them instead of the expensive

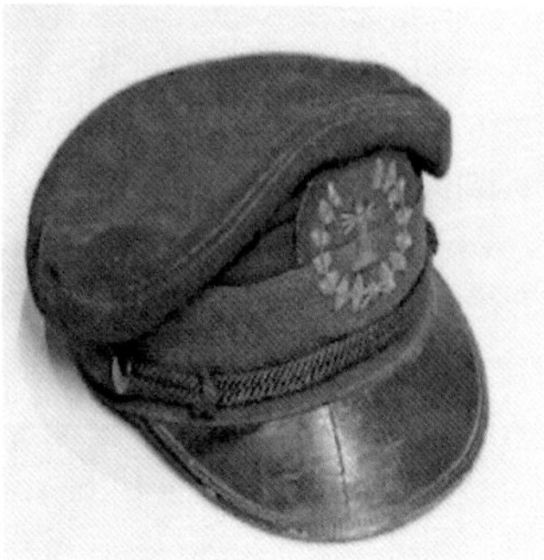

Above: A light keeper's hat. *From* Bruckhaus and Efron Encyclopedic Dictionary, *1890.*

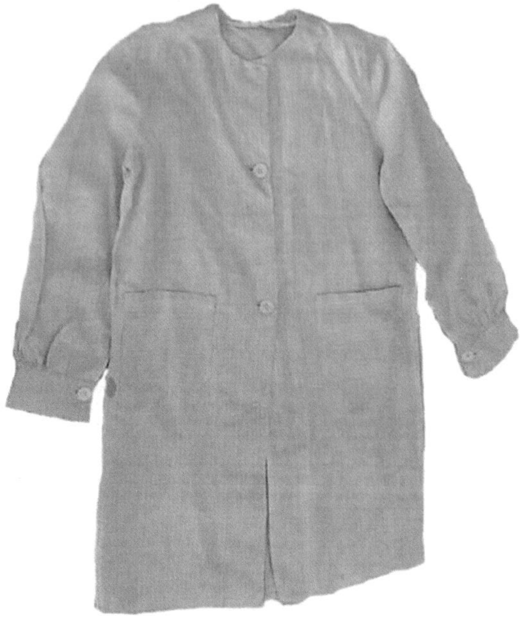

Right: A linen smock worn by keepers to clean lighthouse lenses. *From* Bruckhaus and Efron Encyclopedic Dictionary, *1890.*

uniforms. The smock was made from finely patterned linen of high quality, usually with two bone buttons on the side and on the bottom.

Most keepers quickly found that this was not the only reason the Lighthouse Service required the smock. A close reading of the regulations revealed that in addition, no jewelry, belt buckles, sharp objects or watches were allowed in the lantern room or other vulnerable areas of the lighthouse. A hard and fast rule was that when work was being done in the lens area, keepers had to wear the smock and keep it firmly closed at all times to protect the lens from being scratched while the keeper was working. The glass was the true heart of the lighthouse, and as such, if it were scratched or chipped, it would lose its effectiveness.

The inspectors, of course, found that most keepers handled their duties quite well, even if they occasionally became bored. In some cases, after reading the daily logs, they noted that some keepers appeared to lose their marbles. This was unquestionably due in part to the inspector's ultimate job assignment and his huge responsibility to protect the lighthouse itself, plus the ships and crews that sailed the lakes and oceans. His assessment of the keeper was as critical as his assessment of the lighthouse itself.

A lighthouse most often became a family operation where a husband-and-wife team learned to make the work at the light a shared venture. The husband, as keeper, took full responsibility for the light itself, and the wife took charge of the dwelling. Usually, the whole family then shared the work on the grounds. Many times, the inspectors took advantage of this situation in their respective comments to both. Using a team effort, the inspector would pull the husband aside and tell him that he was doing a fine job but that his wife was letting him down a bit. She just was not keeping the quarters up as expected by the inspector. He would suggest that the keeper, in a nice way, see if she could improve. When the inspector talked with the wife, he would compliment her on the dwelling and casually reflect that the husband might do a better job on the light itself.

While tracing the history of the beautiful old Presque Isle Light, I found story after story told by old salts about the special appeal this lighthouse appears to have and about how its light saved many lives over the years. To many sailors, it became their guiding light and spawned a special intrigue in their lives. From what I have been able to determine from old records and writings, there are many stories about the keepers' lives and the families who cared for it and the many local children who played on the grounds of the lighthouse.

> *Nothing moves the imagination quite like a lighthouse.*
>
> —*Samuel Adams Drake*

I soon found that there was a sort of lingering allure about it. I sometimes think about the first time I decided to visit the site. It was a quiet weekday morning with bright summer sunshine reflecting off Lake Erie and virtually no wind. As I began to walk the area, I felt an enduring tranquility beginning to seep into my psyche. I still cannot wholly explain what I felt. Maybe it was just the way the old light sits even today. The light seems to let visitors effortlessly slide into the past. Even now, when I look out from the lighthouse over the harbor and its entrance, I find myself imagining what the look and feel must have been back in the early 1800s.

Friends who have walked the lighthouse grounds tell me that they, too, can almost see the light keeper and his family living in the original three-room dwelling on the property. Keepers, like Bone, allowed their many children to use the large grounds as a playground, always warning them to stay away from the cliffs down to the lake. At the time, there was a steep path that led down to the perilous rocks and water below where a few fishing shanties dotted the shoreline, with six or more fishing vessels always anchored just offshore. Most keepers monitored who could use this path.

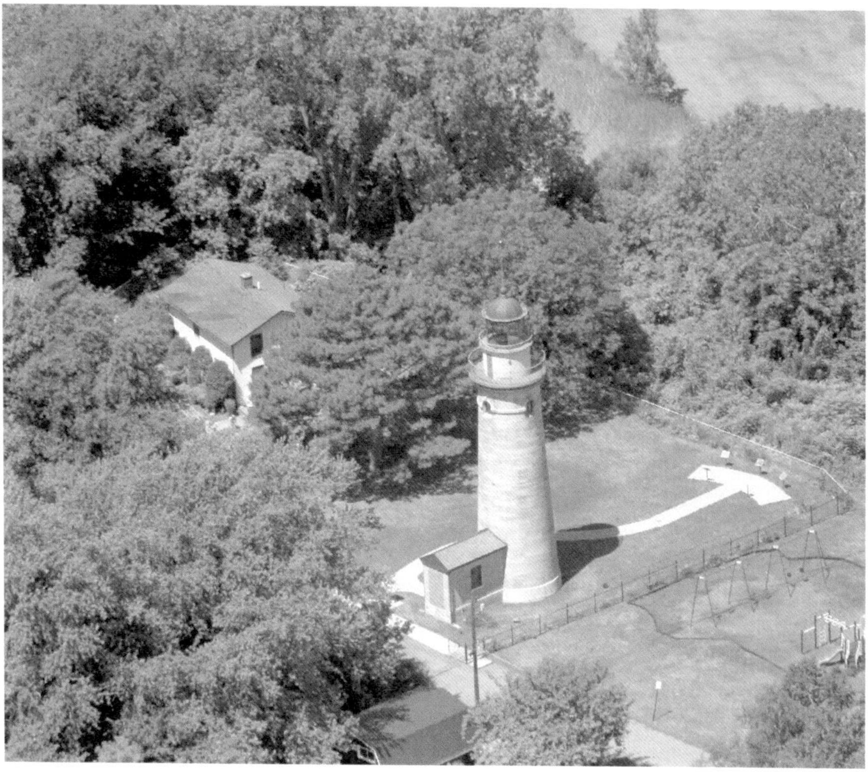

This is a 1960 aerial view of the Erie Land Lighthouse. *Courtesy of Pennsylvania DCNR files.*

> *Lighthouse keepers, like cowboys and pirates, continue to fascinate us though their time has passed.*
>
> —*Robert Sheira, historian*

Back in 1820, the grounds contained many large oak and maple trees. None grew between the old light and the water so that the light's beam could be seen out over the lake. The keeper trimmed all the trees, whether behind or to the sides of the light, on a regular basis. If you were to go to the site today, you would find that the lighthouse is only sixty or so feet back from where the cliffs were at one time. You will also see the cliffs now are more like sloping banks or hills down to the lake. Over the years, the cliffs have slowly eroded and have fallen into the lake, forming a gradual hill, virtually eliminating any of the old cliffs. This has helped preserve and protect the lighthouse, but one problem with the hill structure, even back in the late 1800s, was that trees soon began to grow on the now sloping hillside. This became a major problem for the then active lighthouse.

In 1838, when an inspector from Washington visited the lighthouse, he found the station in good shape and considered the light to be "one of the most useful on the southern shore of the lake." He did make a comment that it shared one problem with many lighthouses of the time: the lamp chimneys were so short that they did not reach above the scallops of the reflectors. That caused soot to collect on these reflectors, reducing their effectiveness. He suggested more frequent cleaning and indicated that he believed thought should be given to changing the lamp system used to a more modern one.

When the original lighthouse was built, it was constructed on wet and soft sandy soil and, due to budget constraints, with just a simple stone foundation. These factors would, in the not too distant future, make the donated land a serious problem. Due to the shallowness of the foundation and the extremely sandy and constantly damp soil, the tower began to sink and lean like the Tower of Pisa after about twenty-five years. In 1851, inspectors from

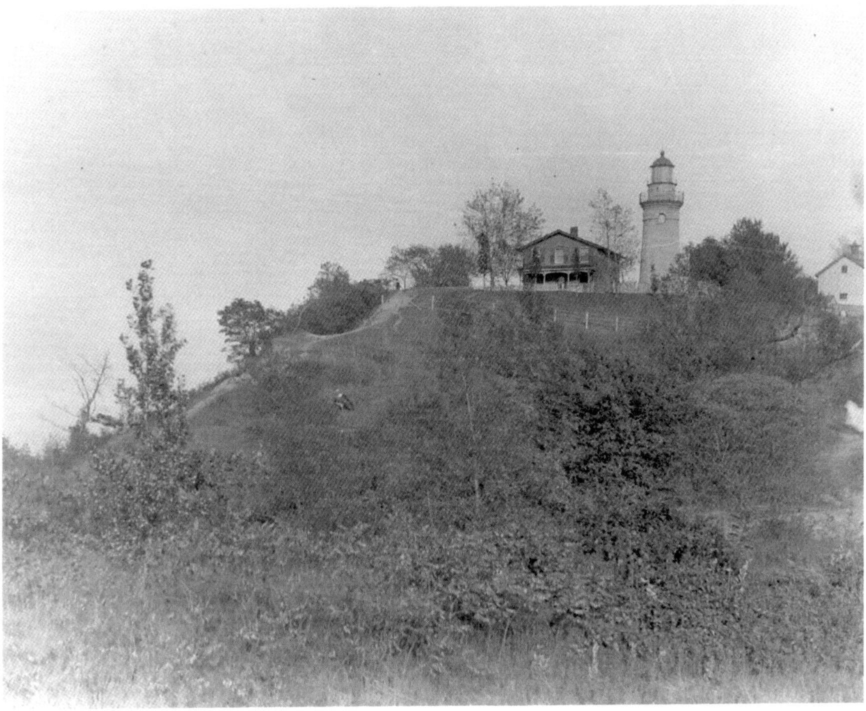

An 1894 view of the Land Lighthouse with the keeper's house, barn and the path to the lake visible. *Courtesy of the Erie County Historical Society.*

Washington ordered metal bands to be placed around the tower to help stabilize it. This did not work, and no other solutions seemed feasible, so by 1856, it was obvious that the tower itself would need to be replaced.

After discussion among local, state and federal authorities, it was decided to move the location of a new lighthouse to the east on what they believed was more stable ground. In 1857, before the original tower actually toppled, construction was begun on a completely new lighthouse. The new lighthouse was designed to be fifty-six feet in height and round. It was also to be nearly twice the diameter of the first tower and was constructed of Milwaukee brick. This brick—also known as "Cream City brick"—was a light yellow brick made from the clay around Milwaukee, Wisconsin, and was used for many lighthouses at the time. The foundation for this new lighthouse was the same as the first lighthouse, except that an additional eighteen inches of stone were added to the foundation base.

The use of what the locals referred to as "imported bricks" infuriated a large group of local citizens who all thought that bricks of local manufacture were of better quality, lower cost and incurred little or no shipping expense.

New Lighthouse Dimensions

Height	fifty-six feet	
Staircase	spiral cast iron	
Number of stairs	seventy-eight	
Tower	top	eighteen feet
	interior	ten feet, three inches
	bottom	twenty-three feet
Lantern room	sixteen feet, five inches	

Looking back, this whole adventure was a good example of why irregularities and mismanagement haunted the reign of Superintendent of Lights Stephen Pleasonton's thirty-two years as head of this service. He ordered that the Milwaukee bricks be used, and it has been estimated that they were twice the price of local bricks and were another foolhardy venture by his office.

The engineers assumed they had the sinking problem solved, and a new, better and taller lighthouse was in place and operational. In spite of their best hopes, the soft ground at this new location continued to plague the lighthouse. This new building lasted just ten years. In 1866, it had to be demolished because it, too, had started sinking. Visitors said they would hear strange noises coming from inside the tower within the first three years after it was built. When the tower was finally taken down, they found that the foundation itself had started to crumble. When they later dug down under the foundation, they discovered that there was quicksand directly below the building.

In 1867, a new site in the same area but about two hundred feet east of the second lighthouse was chosen to be the home of still another lighthouse. This time, the builders finally decided to be more careful with the construction. They dug down twenty feet and layered the hole with eight courses of solid, twelve-inch-thick oak timbers and coated them with an oil-based tar.They then layered over a ton of finely crushed limestone on top and let it settle before covering it with Portland cement. When that had settled, a two-and-a-half-inch-thick covering of concrete was poured, and eight more inches of crushed stone were added before the final foundation was laid. Now, the Lighthouse Service was ready to build the third and final lighthouse.

At the last minute, the Lighthouse Service decided to replace the proposed exterior brick with Berea sandstone. It was hoped that the lighter, yet very durable, sandstone would be a good substitute for the brick. It worked; the third lighthouse became the last.

When this version of the light was built, a third-order Fresnel lens was installed (see Chapter 4 for more on Fresnel lenses). Kerosene fueled the beacon itself and displayed a fixed white light from a covered lamp room structure. The balcony, where the lantern room sat, was a little over 16 feet wide. The lighthouse with its new lens had a focal plane of 128 feet above Lake Erie and could be seen about fifteen to seventeen miles offshore.

On March 3, 1871, Congress appropriated funds to raise the roof of the keeper's dwelling to provide a second floor. Many other renovations were

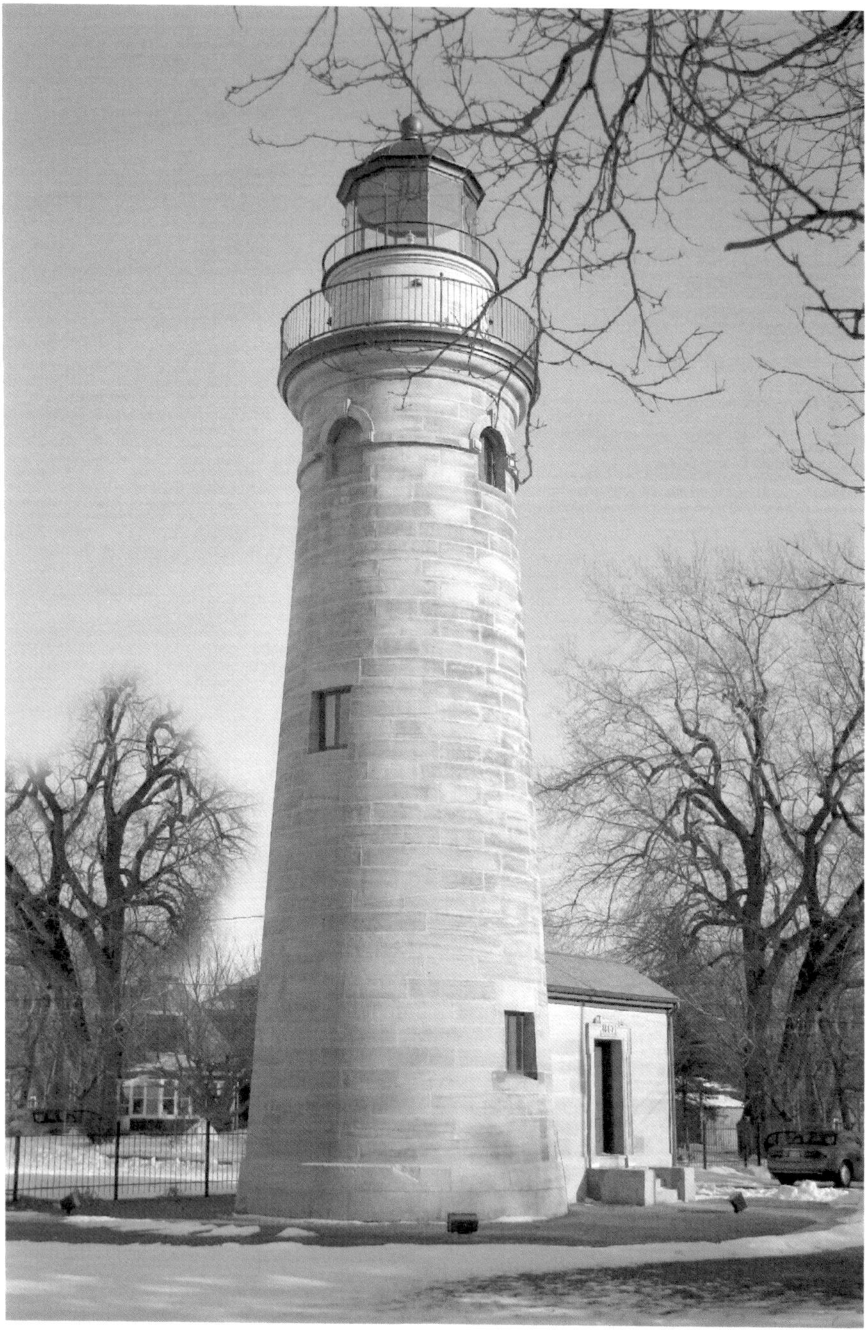

A photograph of the Erie Land Lighthouse shortly after the City of Erie renovations around 1959. *Courtesy of Pennsylvania DCNR files.*

also made at the same time, including adding new brickwork around the windows of both the light and dwelling. A barn on the property was also refurbished at that time.

However, even back in the late 1800s, many bureaucrats were silently stealing through the halls of government. It was late in 1880 that Commander G.W. Howard of the Tenth Lighthouse District, under the cloaking cover of the winter season, when the light was not in active service, ordered the lighthouse to be decommissioned and sold at auction.

One of the strange facts involved with this situation was that neither he nor even any of his staff had ever been to Erie to visit the lighthouse. He also never bothered to consult or inform any local officials. Howard then went on to sell it for just $1,800 within ninety days. On March 1, 1881, a citizen named Myron Sanford, who owned adjoining property, purchased the lighthouse, forcing its closing. It has been estimated that the long-term cost to the Lighthouse Board of this closing was between $28,000 and $30,000.

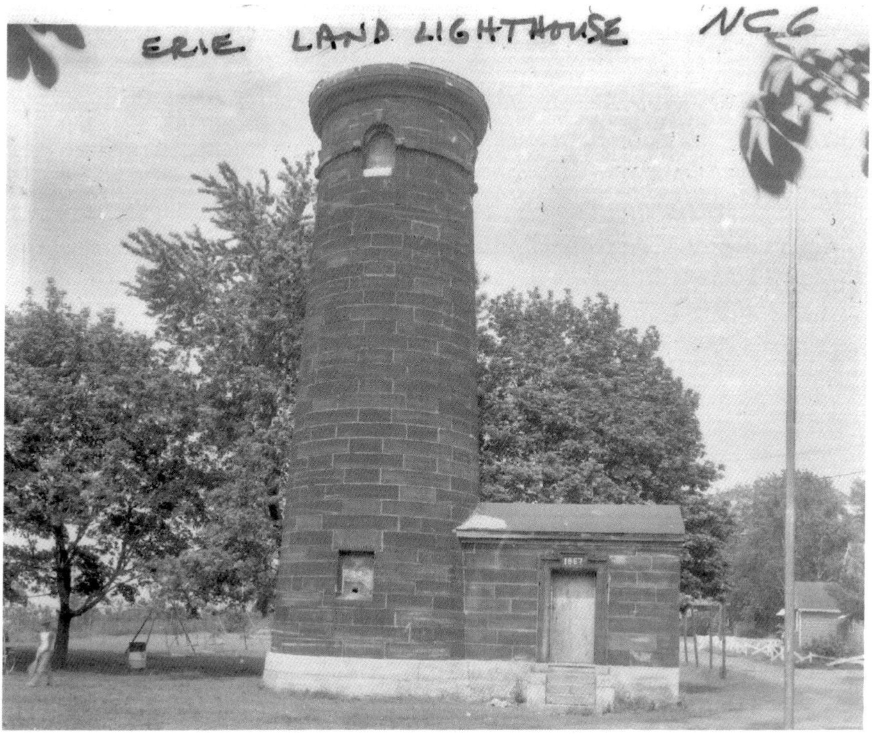

The Land Lighthouse with no lamp room at the top of the tower during a period when maintenance by the City of Erie was needed. *Courtesy of the Erie County Historical Society.*

When the citizens of Erie, shippers and mariners became aware of what was happening with their lighthouse, they became outraged. On July 7, 1884, during the very next full session of Congress, a bill was quickly passed to buy the lighthouse back and restore it to service. This little bureaucratic misadventure of having to now buy the lighthouse back cost the Lighthouse Board an additional amount of between $7,500 and $25,000, depending on how the cost is calculated. This, needless to say, would have been many years of operating expense for the Presque Isle Light had it not been sold.

The problems, of course, did not end with the congressional action. In the long period of reopening the lighthouse, a full-time custodian and watchman were needed to protect the property from "tramps," which also incurred more costs. It was soon found that most of the metalwork and other key parts were in storage in a warehouse at Buffalo, New York. Once the equipment was found, it was discovered that it was in extremely bad condition. When it was to be transported back to Erie, it was found that many pieces were missing while some of the others were damaged beyond repair. All these missing or damaged parts needed to be repaired, replaced or refabricated in order to get the light reopened. This unexpected delay lasted until July 1, 1885, when a new light was installed in the tower. It had a new revolving third-order Fresnel lens and was first exhibited from the tower when it finally reopened.

Eventually, even the local population and mariners began to realize that the onward and continuous eastward march of Presque Isle now simply made the beautiful old lighthouse nearly invisible to most ships coming to the harbor from any direction other than the northeast. In addition, now that the new flash light was open on Presque Isle, the venerable old lady, now renamed Erie Land Lighthouse, was no longer really needed as a functioning lighthouse.

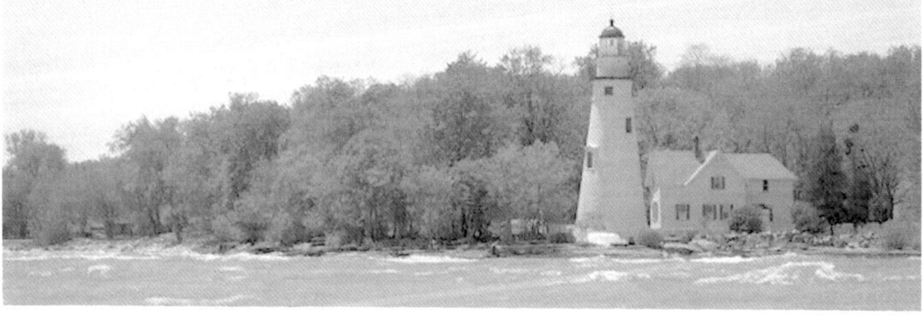

Marblehead Light in Sandusky, Ohio, home of the Erie Land Lighthouse Fresnel lens. *Courtesy of the U.S. Coast Guard.*

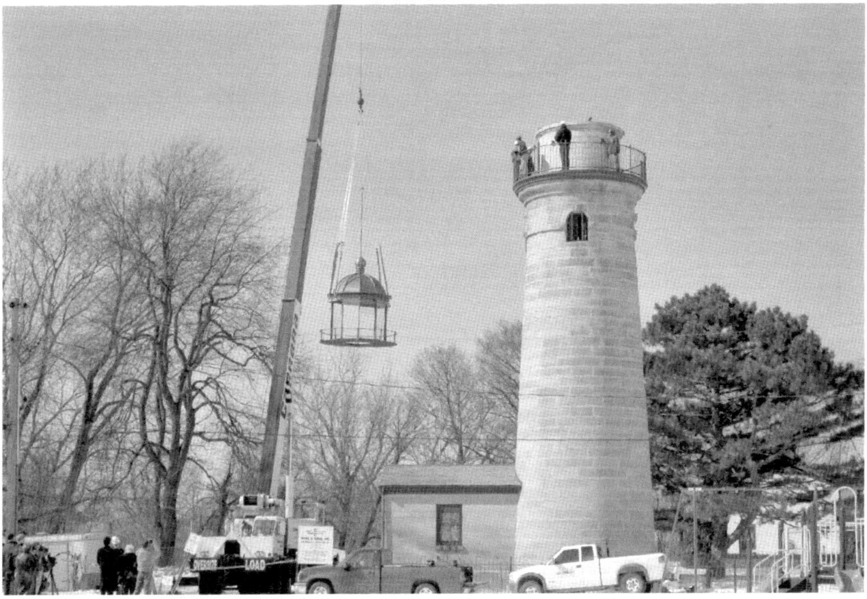

The new lamp room is being lifted into place during the Erie Land Lighthouse restoration in the late 1950s. *Courtesy of Jerry Skrypzak.*

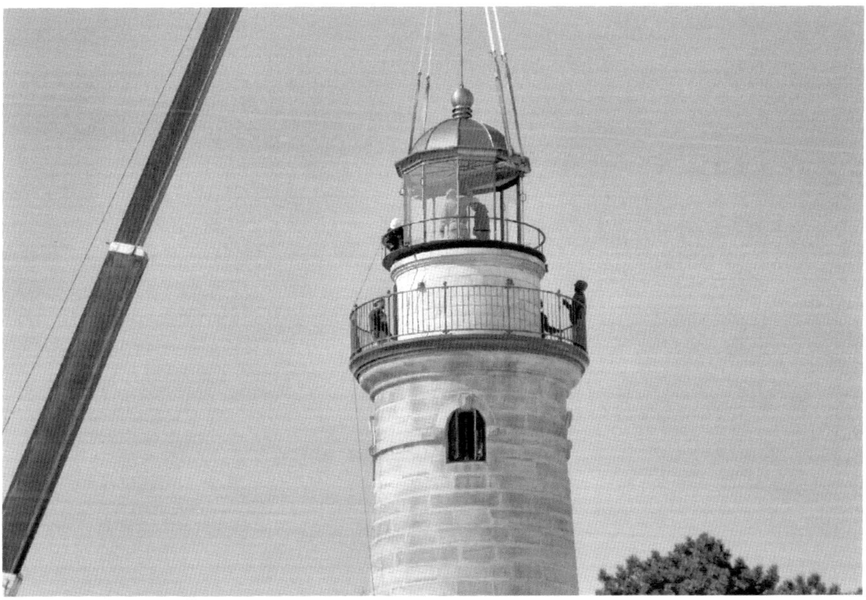

The final connection of the lamp room to the Erie Land Lighthouse. *Courtesy of Jerry Skrypzak.*

Finally, in 1899, after little debate, the light was considered obsolete and deactivated. The Fresnel lens was transferred to the Marblehead Light in Sandusky, Ohio. Marblehead—which was built in 1821, just three years after the Erie Land Lighthouse—is today the oldest continuously operating lighthouse on the Great Lakes. Its sixty-five-foot tower still spreads its green light out over Lake Erie.

In the end, the final reason the light was closed was because Presque Isle kept moving eastward each year, and the large trees that were growing on the cliffs now blocked much of the lighthouse. These facts irrevocably doomed the light. Of course, the new Presque Isle Light Station and the North Pier Light with their excellent locations more than made up for the loss of this old honored light.

Ownership of the Erie Land Lighthouse remained with the federal government until 1934, when the lighthouse was transferred to the City of Erie. After sitting dormant for many years, the city, with the help of many private citizens, restored the light. The Erie Land Lighthouse, its lamp room, the keeper's house and the grounds have now become a popular and beautiful historic site.

4

FROM SMOKE, WHALE OIL AND MIRRORS TO THE BIRTH OF THE FRESNEL LENS

I remember the first time I saw what I now know was a third-order Fresnel (the *s* is silent) lens. In 1978, when our family decided to take a vacation, we spent a week in Bar Harbor and Boothbay, Maine, before traveling down to Cape Cod for a week. One morning, I wandered into a rather small and dusty maritime museum in Boothbay. The family was, of course, gathering at the local gift shop. Climbing the stairs just off the entrance, I wandered into a rather out-of-the-way room on the second floor.

There I saw what looked to me like a very large and strange glittering contraption. The whole display was slowly turning on a walnut base with a candle-like glow coming through the glass. The glow covered the entire room with an intricate pattern of sparkling light. Immediately, I began to develop a feeling of vertigo. Even so, I thought the room and object were captivatingly beautiful. However, I had no idea what I was looking at or how it might have been used. Although being in an ocean seaport, I surmised it must be a lens of some sort and was likely used within one of the nearby lighthouses. Walking up to the display, I read the signage on the cabinet. It explained that it was a lens used in a lighthouse and gave a brief outline of the life of the inventor, Augustin Fresnel. That was many years ago, and until I started the research on this book, I had not revisited Fresnel's story or his invention.

I remember looking more carefully at the display and found that it had hundreds of finely polished prisms of thick cut-glass placed in distinct locations by someone with precise skills to form a perfect series of patterns.

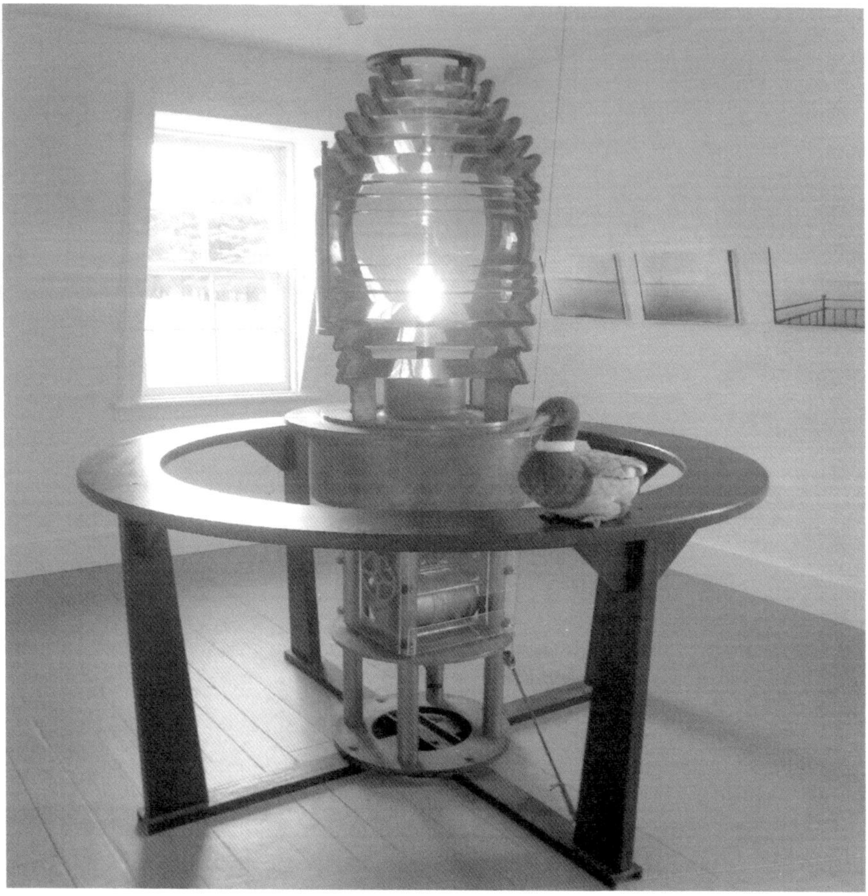

A Fresnel lens in an old Maine maritime museum. *Author's collection.*

The lens seemed to have an ingenious way of completely capturing my undivided attention. It appeared to me to have a unique design, unlike anything I had ever seen before. There was a pointed top, and it was covered with many individual glass panels. Some of the panels looked like they had unanticipated soap bubbles within them. I am sure that is what gave me the vertigo feeling and also made the light rays appear to shimmer as they exited the lens.

The panels and a few thick glass crystals, some looking like gemstones, were looped together by a slim brass network of securing bridgework. This made me think that, over time, keeping this brass polished and bright must have been an almost full-time job. It was the only display in that room, yet I knew instantly it was all that was ever going to be needed here to mesmerize any who entered that room.

Before Fresnel lenses became the worldwide standard, many other ways to propel light deep out to sea were sought. Some worked fairly well; others were total disasters. The Pharos of Alexandria (see the preface) was said to have a fire at its top and a huge curved mirror to reflect the fire's light far out to sea. It was said that if one looked into the mirror, ships could be seen a great distance from shore. Just across the Mediterranean, the Roman Empire was erecting similarly mirrored lighthouses using highly polished metal sheets. This was fine until the Roman Empire failed, and most of their lights just went out of service.

After the fall of the Roman Empire, much of the European and Mediterranean coastlines went dark. This may have been a good thing because Viking warships prowled the waters looking for the lights that would show them the population centers. Between AD 800 and AD 1100, the Vikings were the best sailors in the world, but history shows they built no lighthouses or permanent coastal lights. The advancement of the lighthouse began with new vigor in 1300 and moved throughout the Mediterranean Sea and the Atlantic coast of Portugal, Spain, France and England. From mid-1300 to 1450, France became the world's greatest sailing power. Navigators such as Jacques Cartier and Samuel de Champlain led the way across the seas to North America. With this expansion of the French influence, King Henry III of France ordered the building of many new lighthouses along the French coast to support the thriving wine trade and other expansionist ventures the country was developing. When the seventeenth century came, it brought with it a considerable acceleration in lighthouse development in many other nations of Europe that bordered the oceans.

In researching this book, I asked myself many times what were the various forms of light used over the centuries in the early lighthouses or light towers? The answer, of course, is many different forms. Many early light towers had large bonfires either on their tops or beneath them. In France, towns and villages would build huge bonfires on the beaches near harbor entrances to indicate their location to ships at sea. These lights were not very useful but were better than nothing. Some were fitted with a convex mirror to reflect the light upward, and others had mirror-like devices to direct the beams out to sea. Following this, in the Renaissance era and for three centuries after its end, the use of specialized and varied candles became the normal way to produce the light for lighthouses. These early lamps or fires used in the lighthouses were dirty, sooty, produced toxic fumes and were hard to keep burning in drafty conditions. In addition to this, they were not very effective as beacons and did not produce any reliable beam.

The most widely used lamp in the 1700s was the spider lamp, which had a shallow, open brass pan as a reservoir plus three or more adjustable wicks that surrounded the pan. Because of poor design, these lamps usually had no chimneys, were exceptionally dirty and at times were incredible fire hazards due to the oil reservoir and its placement.

By the mid-1700s, the contemporary technology in lighthouse optics consisted of single or multiple oil-burning lamps in some form of lantern placed at the top of a tower. Some had mirror-like devices mounted behind them. The only way to increase the output of the light was to increase the size of the flame. Again, this was a risky practice and produced only marginal results.

It was not until the mid-eighteenth century that a Frenchman named François Pierre Aimé Argand designed sets of lamps with attendant reflectors that greatly improved the distribution of light from lighthouses. During his early efforts, he soon found that his biggest problem was that light was naturally diffused in a 360-degree arc from the center. Argand also knew that light could be diffused, either with mirrors or naturally, on a horizontal plane and then be sent out to sea where sailors could see it. Unfortunately, nearly 50 percent of the total light was still lost.

A new catoptric system—which he invented in 1781 and then improved over the year—involved either a few or, in some cases, many parabolic reflectors. They were placed on light sources and used to magnify their strength.The benefit of the parabolic shape was that a beam of light emitted from a light source at the focal point of the mirror was always reflected in a horizontal line from any point it would strike on the mirror.

While a great improvement and very workable, it, too, was still extremely inefficient, with no more than 40 percent of the light being transmitted in the right direction. Regrettably, most mariners felt that the light beams were still critically limited. They related to authorities that the light could not be seen more than fifteen miles out to sea even in clear weather. By the time a vessel saw the light, many would have little time to turn away from the looming danger that the light was meant to warn sailors about.

Argand soon realized the main problem he ran into with his early techniques was gaining an effective, bright and reliable light source to match his parabolic reflector system. Therefore, at the same time he worked on the mirror system, he was also working on the development of a new and distinctive oil lamp that he might team with these reflectors/mirrors. Over

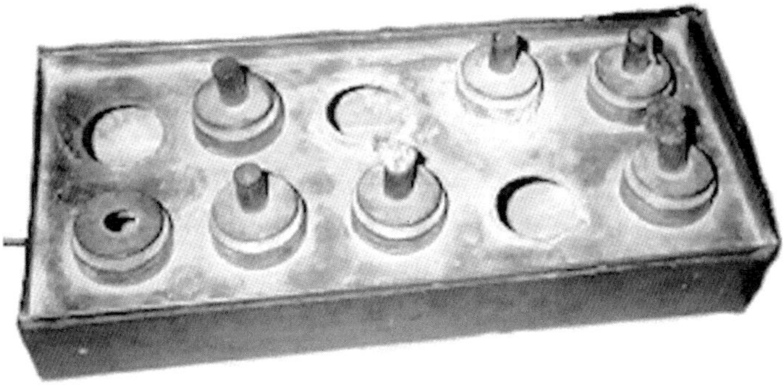

Above: A spider lamp from the early 1800s. *From* Bruckhaus and Efron Encyclopedic Dictionary, *1890.*

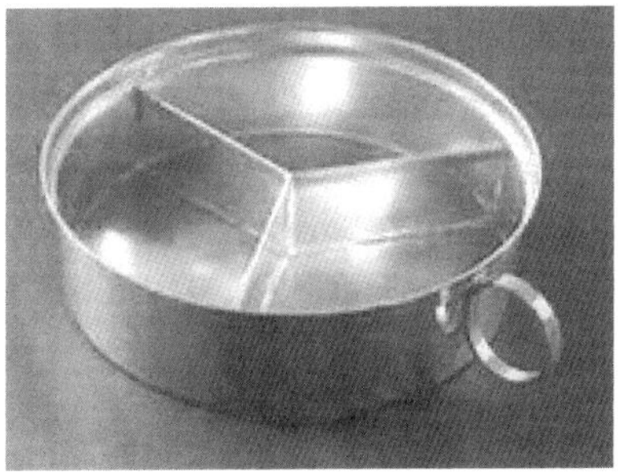

Right: A rouge container used with rouge to clean brass on lenses, 1800s. *From* Bruckhaus and Efron Encyclopedic Dictionary, *1890.*

the years, he refined the design of this lamp until he could gain a much brighter light and still have it be nearly smokeless. This achievement greatly reduced the burden of the light keeper's daily chores.

To make the new lamp work well, it had a hollow, circular wick that allowed oxygen to pass quite evenly on both sides. As Argand soon discovered, if he narrowed the neck of the chimney just above the flame, he could direct the oxygen into the flame and increase the brightness of the light. All of Europe quickly adopted Argand's lamp system, and the lives of the light keepers improved tremendously. He later found that keeping the reserve of oil above the combustion chamber gave a better flow of oil to the wick.

As mentioned in the previous chapter, in 1810, Argand was soon to gather a new world competitor: Winslow Lewis. He was a former sea captain. He freely borrowed much of Argand's technology. With the help of his father-in-law, a noted mathematical instrument maker who specialized in navigation, he began to develop a new form of lamp and reflector. In just a few years, they came up with a new system. The design of the lamp was nearly the same as that patented by Argand in 1780. Very few of the Argand lamps made it into lighthouses in the United States. As I mentioned earlier, the old spider lamp was the lamp of choice here until the 1810–14 period. However, as the new lamps became available, they began to replace the unsafe spider lamps.

The one advantage the Lewis lamp had over the old lamps in use in the United States was that it burned only 50 percent of the oil then in use at the operational lighthouses. The following year, Lewis was offered an exclusive contract to outfit all the U.S. lighthouses. In the end, they gave him $60,000 for the patent, the refitting of the lighthouses and the maintenance of them for the next seven years. To complete the contract, Lewis had to guarantee that his lamps would use half the whale oil as the old lamps. He was able to do this based on an unexpected extension of the time frame owing to the beginning of the War of 1812.

Sometime around 1816, he signed another contract to continue the light maintenance of all United States lighthouses. The new arrangement was based on his cutting the amount of oil needed by the same 50 percent as his old contract. The government would deliver the specified amount of oil, and if any were left over, he could sell it on the open market and keep any profit. Over the years of the contract, it proved to be a very profitable provision, because his average oil sales were $12,000 per year. Back in those days, that amounted to nearly four years' salary for a federal employee.

With shipping increasing worldwide, many realized that an optical system that could cast light many more miles out to sea was desperately needed. Such a system could save lives and loss of cargo, plus stop many shipwrecks and make commerce more straightforward and thus more profitable for merchants and suppliers.

In 1819, the French government commissioned thirty-four-year-old Augustin-Jean Fresnel to develop an improved lighting system for all French lighthouses. A well-known and accomplished engineer and scientist, Fresnel had worked for years to change the accepted understanding of how light behaved and how it could be manipulated and then intensified. His insistence that most other scientists were wrong in how they viewed light rays angered many in Europe for most of the early 1800s. In the end, his revolutionary systems of lens optics replaced the old practice of using multiple parabolic reflectors and lamp assemblies.

He first started his work by ignoring the reflector standard and began investigating the various ways that glass lenses could be manipulated to concentrate the light source and project it where he wanted it to go. The first thing he realized was that a single lens of sufficient strength would need to be huge and, for this reason, was not practical.

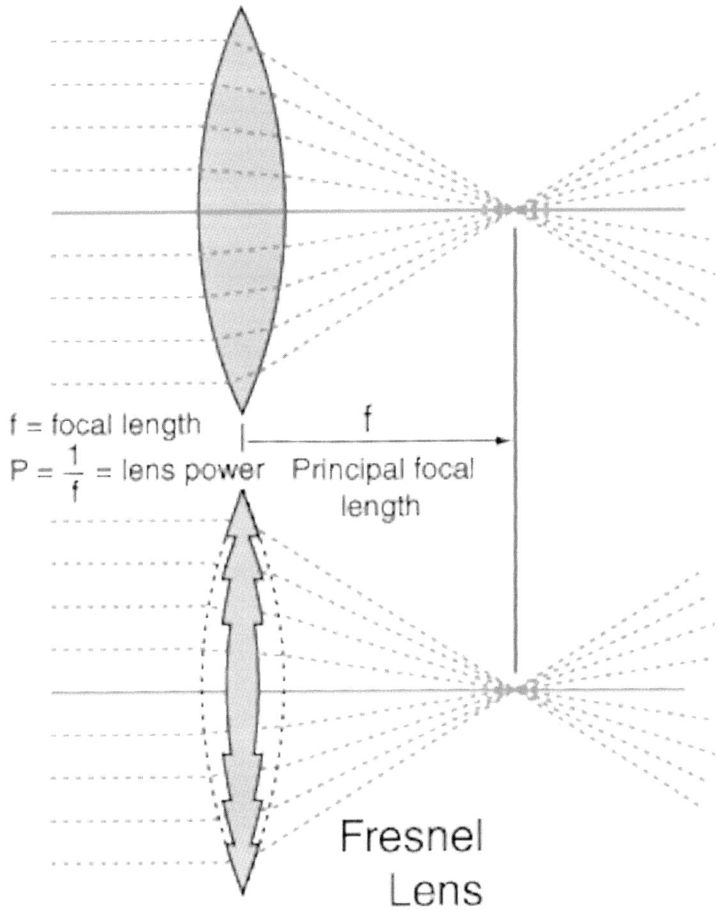

A drawing of a Fresnel lens's rays. *Courtesy of Wikimedia Commons.*

As he worked on the project, he encountered many other scientists who believed that he was a maverick with slightly crazy ideas. Most of them felt he should go back to designing bridges and highways, where he had gotten most of his practical experience. However, using a simple, ingenious form, Fresnel's design ended up being a multi-row, barrel-shaped array of various types of lenses surrounding a strong light source.

In all his lenses, in the area immediately horizontal to the light source, dioptric (refracting) lenses magnified and concentrated the light as it passed

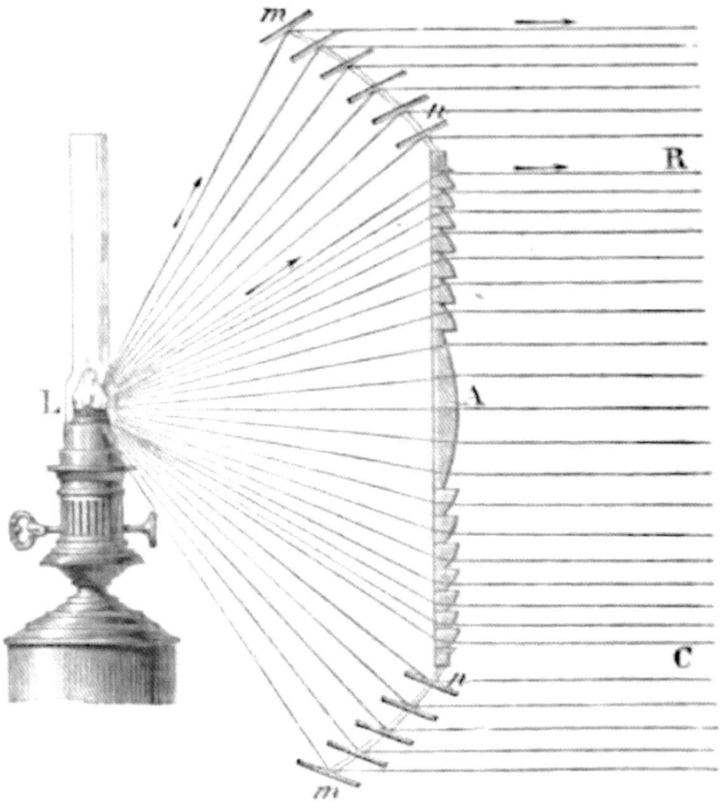

A diagram of a Fresnel lens. *Courtesy of Wikimedia Commons.*

through them. In the same array, usually above and below the center lenses and light source, multiple catadioptric prisms (lenses and prisms where refraction and reflection are combined) were mounted around the periphery of the barrel. Each of these many prisms collected and intensified the light and redirected it to the same plane as the dioptric lenses. Most Fresnel lenses had the ability to transmit 80 to 85 percent of the light collected. This was a dramatic increase over the old systems.

If you look at a Fresnel lens logically, you will find the basic theory behind it very simple. Just take a magnifying glass lens and slice it into a hundred concentric rings, similar to the rings of a tree. Now view each ring in a slightly thinner version of the one before it and focus it toward the center. Next, take each ring and modify it so that it is flat on one side yet the same thickness as all the others. In order to retain the ring's capability to focus the light to a specific point, the angle of each ring must be set in a slightly different position. When all lenses are stacked back together, you have the principle of a Fresnel lens.

Fresnel soon found that by rotating the optic array, thousands of different possibilities of color and flash patterns could be obtained. Using the dioptric or bull's-eye panels that were around the central panels of the array, each light could be made to flash in different, easily identifiable characteristic patterns and could be made to show alternating colors.

One significant advantage of the Fresnel lens was that it could be manufactured at one location, tested and disassembled and shipped to its final location and easily reassembled. This also could allow the flash patterns and color to be changed simply by changing out the bull's-eye panels.

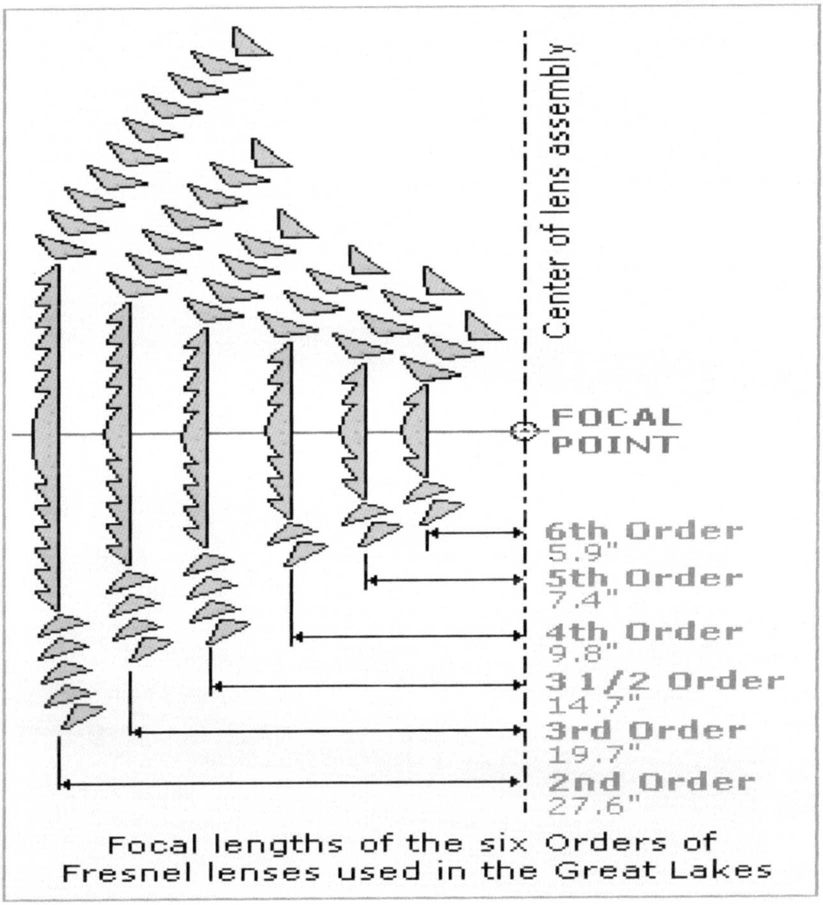

A comparison of Fresnel lenses. *Courtesy of Wikimedia Commons.*

Another advantage was that the speed of the rotation could be changed without difficulty. There were a number of ways that the Fresnel lenses could be rotated; however, the one preferred by Fresnel himself used a mercury floatation system to reduce friction and vibration when the lenses were revolving. To make the float system work, he attached a ring-shaped base to the lens, and the combined unit was submerged and floated on a basin containing two or more gallons of mercury. This system provided a nearly frictionless method of turning the lens, which also allowed for a much faster and easily varied rate of rotation.

The problem with this was that mercury happened to be a dangerous material to the keeper and his family due to its horrible toxicity. What was not well known in the 1800s was that a gram of mercury can produce

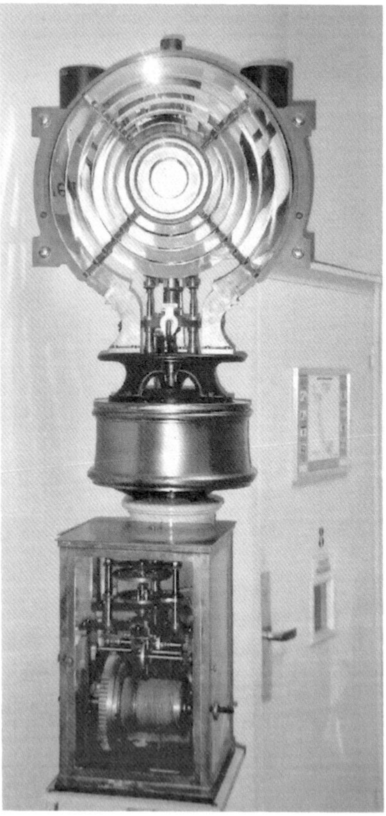

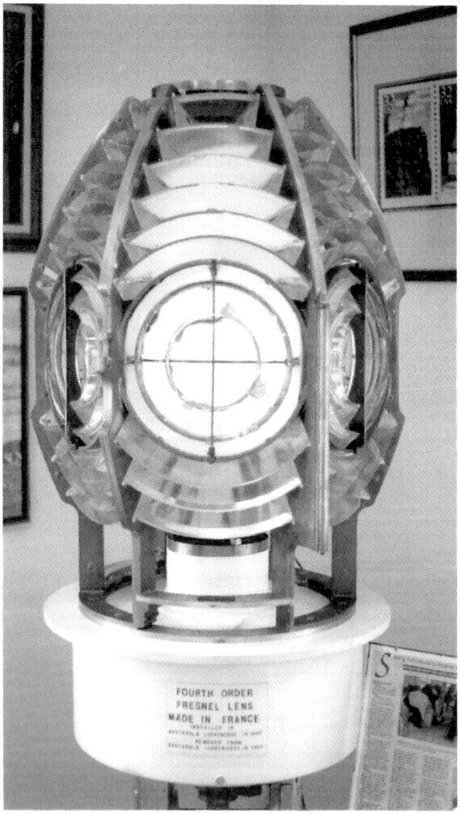

Left: The first turning unit using the mercury float system in a lighthouse on the French coast. *From* Bruckhaus and Efron Encyclopedic Dictionary, *1890.*

Right: The Ashtabula, Ohio lighthouse mercury float unit. *Courtesy of Wikimedia Commons.*

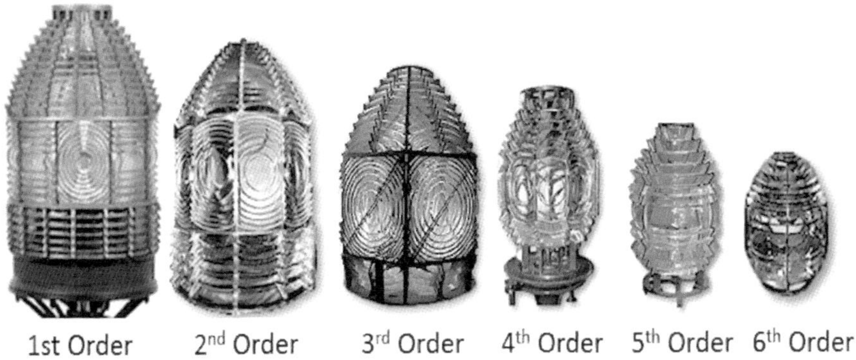

Fresnel lens sizes. *Courtesy of Wikimedia Commons.*

high toxicity or death. Mercury poisoning can result in several diseases that have effects on the brain, lungs and kidneys. It has been shown to impair vision, hearing, coordination and speech. The use of mercury in lighthouses continued until 1920, when most rotation mechanisms were replaced. Over the years, many governments and private groups have made efforts to regulate the use of mercury and to constantly issue advisories about its use.

Unfortunately, American lighthouses were exceptionally slow in implementing the Fresnel lenses, due in large part to treasury auditor Stephen Pleasonton's resistance to change. Annoyed by angry complaints from sailors and shippers, the federal government authorized a complete study of all the lighthouses. The study found the lighthouses, in general, to be in fairly poor condition. Pleasonton would not allow any badly needed improvements and repairs to the lighthouses, including the installation of any of the new lenses. He was discharged from his position within ninety days of the completion of the study, and the Lighthouse Board was created in 1852 to replace him. By the eve of the Civil War, all American lighthouses were using Fresnel's technology.

The Fresnel lens design eventually was refined to include eleven orders or sizes. Each lens, while distinctly designed and slightly different, featured a standard focal length. Of these eleven orders, only six were used in the lighthouses of the Great Lakes.

5

NORTH PIERHEAD LIGHT

Any story about the North Pierhead Light must be linked closely with the important changes taking place at the entrance to the Erie harbor. As related in Chapter 2, both the federal and state governmental bodies had surveyed the harbor entrance and its problems. They agreed early on, in the 1818–24 period, that something had to be done to open the channel for easier access to Presque Isle Bay.

Even though the new Presque Isle Light on the cliffs east of the town of Erie was now operational, navigation through the harbor channel entrance remained extremely difficult. As in the days of Oliver H. Perry, two long and winding sandbars formed a twisted, shallow route into Presque Isle Bay. In 1819, a federal government survey confirmed that the average depth of the entrance was just six feet.

Another important factor in the entrance problem was the constantly changing channel bottom caused by the shifting sands that were characteristic of Presque Isle. These sands, moved by the prevailing winds and weather on the lake, caused nearly daily changes in the depth of the water and the locations of the sandbars themselves. A study done in 1992 confirmed that the movement and expansion to the east of Presque Isle is still an average of twenty-six feet per year.

It was at some point between 1819 and 1824 that a few citizens of Erie took matters into their own hands. They made a series of crude attempts to construct a channel entrance with hemlock logs and branches. It somewhat worked; however, it had no lasting effect on the problem.

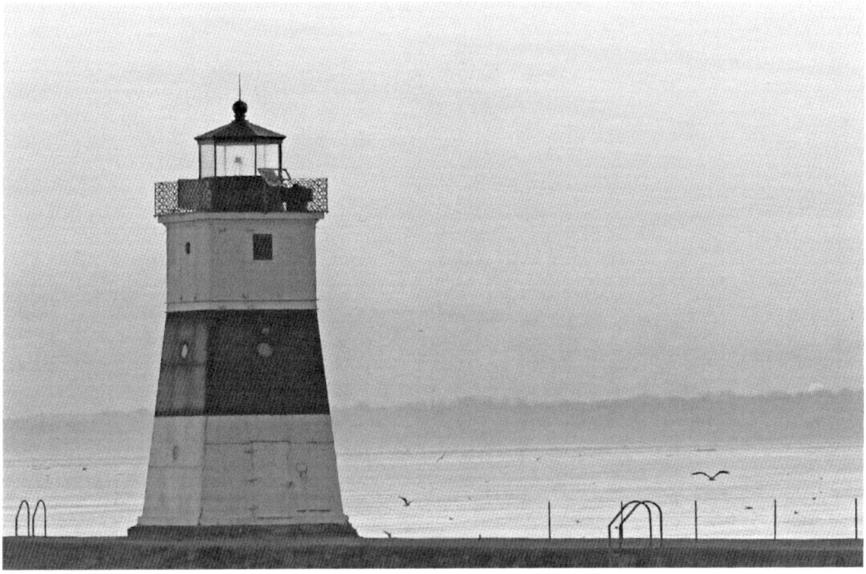

An early afternoon view of North Pierhead Light in 2006. *Author's collection.*

In 1822, the state took over the situation and ordered a new survey. A committee of three local citizens took new readings to ascertain the depth of the waters of the bay, of the channel, on the sandbars and in the anchorage area on the lake. As soon as the state's survey was completed, $15,000 was allocated for improving the harbor.

At this point, Daniel Dobbins used his considerable influence in Washington to gain a series of harbor improvement appropriations to create a viable channel with fixed pier structures and a lighthouse. Shortly after this, in 1824, the federal government decided to handle the sandbar problem, and from that point on, maintaining the channel became its task. That fall, a three-year project was initiated that led to the creation of today's commercial harbor entrance. However, it was not until 1827 that the federal government finally cut through the sandbars and built piers to hold back the shifting sands of Presque Isle. This was the first time a nearly uniform depth was achieved, and a reasonably straight passage into Presque Isle Bay was now possible. Due to the persistence of the businessmen and citizens of Erie, between 1823 and 1894, the state and federal governments invested $827,000 in harbor improvements. Back in those days, this was an enormous amount of money to be spent on a single project.

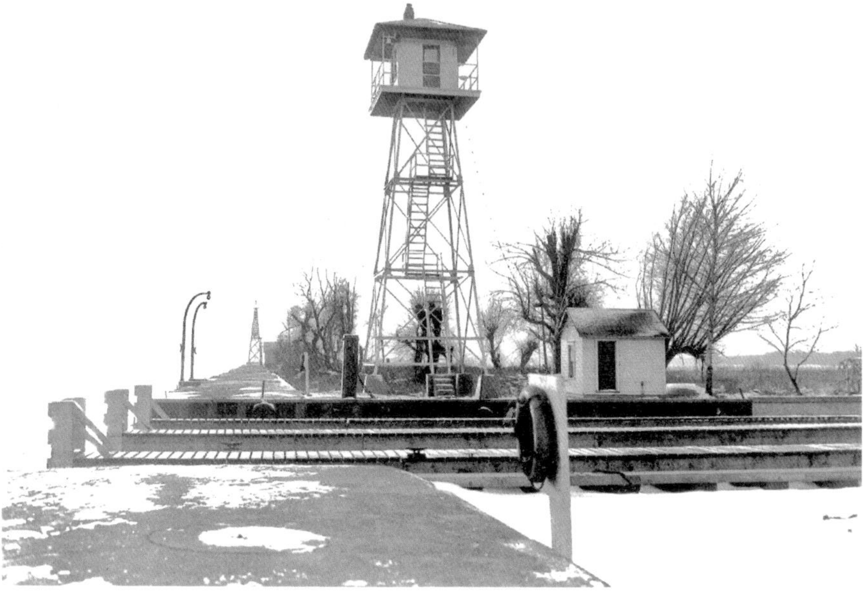

An early view of the light tower situated at the U.S. Coast Guard station in the late 1890s. *Courtesy of Pennsylvania DCNR files.*

A simple octagonal wooden tower beacon was erected in 1828 at the far eastern end of the peninsula pier near the harbor's new entrance. Within two years, a beacon light was placed at the top of the tower. It was powered by whale oil and had to be constantly attended. At the time, it was called the "Tower Beacon Light."

This tower was needed because, even with the new Presque Isle Light east of the city, navigation to the actual channel entrance was still challenging. This was a result of the almost hidden nature of the channel. Sailing toward it at night or dusk was difficult because the channel opening completely blended into the wooded background against which it sat. This setting made finding the channel's actual entrance in the dark nearly impossible.

Mariners used the new light tower to locate the channel against the nearly black shoreline of Presque Isle. In fact, an 1837 federal government report suggested that the Tower Beacon Light was so situated that it usually could not be seen by vessels running down the lake until they were very close to it. The study also went on to suggest to vessels that they use the Presque Isle Light Station on the cliffs to gain the upper entrance to the harbor and then follow the Tower Beacon Light to the channel.

By 1833, there was a respectable channel with a depth of twelve to fourteen feet from the lake into Presque Isle Bay. This depth was maintained until 1839. Then the federal government, now satisfied that most of the problems were past, suspended work in the Erie harbor. In 1833, Rufus Reed, who had anticipated such a governmental move and was worried about keeping the channel open to traffic, used his significant power and influence to get himself appointed superintendent of the peninsula. He felt that at least now he would have something to say about all actions taken by the government. At that time, Presque Isle was assumed to be under the jurisdiction of the City of Erie. However, this authority was not clear. Most people recognized that Reed's actions were targeted at protecting his own interests in the harbor and shipping. However, many people soon found that this was only partially true. His first action was to establish rules against settling on Presque Isle, logging, burning or picking cranberries. In those days, Presque Isle was abundant with the wild berries. During his time as superintendent, he was successful in getting much-needed work done in the channel and harbor. In 1844, a new survey was taken of the channel area, and it was found that the piers were in dilapidated condition; however, there was a depth of nearly

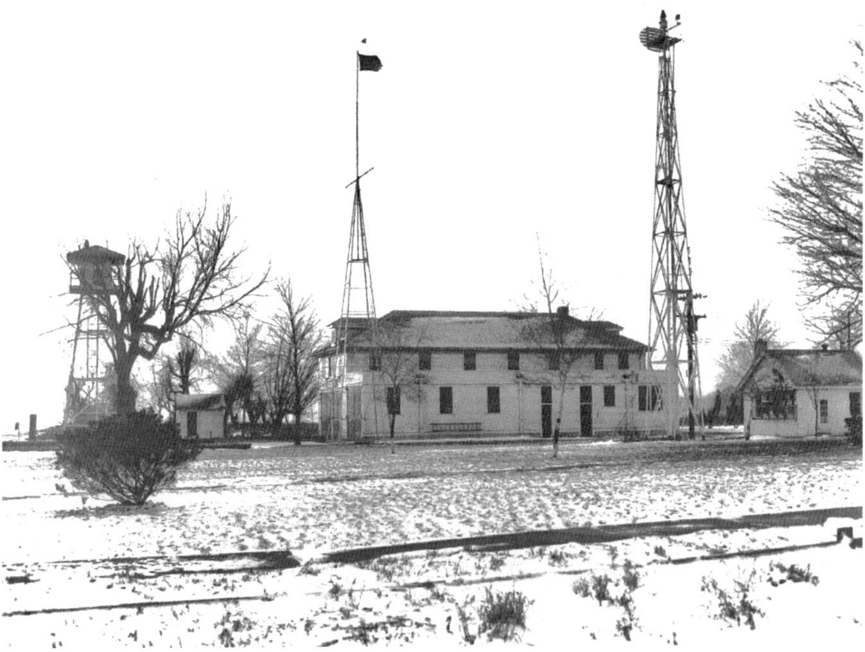

The U.S. Coast Guard station and towers in 1899. *Courtesy of Pennsylvania DCNR files.*

eighteen feet between them. It was noted in the survey that sand shoals were forming at each end of the channel, and the light tower itself needed some updating and immediate repairs. Reed, in his new position, used it to lobby both federal and state agencies for continued support for the harbor.

From 1845 to 1855, a small amount of dredging of the forming sand shoals was undertaken. In addition, some general repairs were made to the light, yet the light continued to be operated far below normal conditions. This kept its two keepers busy around the clock during the shipping season on Lake Erie. Traffic in and out of the port was growing rapidly, with fishing now becoming a huge new industry for the town. The lighting methods used in the Tower Light were described at the time as being "very defective." Ship captains complained to anyone they thought might influence government officials to do something about the need for more and better lights on the approaches to Presque Isle Bay and its protected harbor. In addition to this, the light keepers all constantly complained that the continued use of whale oil made more work because it made for heavy lifting, and they had to constantly tend the lamps.

It was not until 1854 that someone listened to the keepers' problems and the Tower Light received a catadioptric apparatus that included a sixth-order Fresnel lens. This new equipment illuminated an arc of just over 270 degrees and was able to throw the light a much greater distance. This helped solve the problem of visibility of the light from the tower but did not help the light keepers' workload.

At the same time, the Lighthouse Board also adopted the existing range lights that served as markers for mariners entering the harbor. Range lights can be lighted or not lighted. The buoys used in the 1850s were not lighted and were considered lateral markers, which functioned as an early warning and guided vessels into the channel entrance proper. They were red and green and still mark channel entrances around the world. The red buoys mark the port or left side of the channel when sailing toward land. These markers had previously been privately maintained by the many fishermen and tug operators. A range light list in 1856 shows that there were three range beacons in use at Erie: one on the west end of the pier and two on the peninsula, northeast of the pier itself.

These improvements lasted just over one year until the schooner *Pilgrim's Progress* ran up and over the pier during a stormy gale. The accident destroyed both the beacon and its new lens. Many believed that it was not just the gale that caused the disaster; the healthy dose of rum consumed by the captain may have helped it along.

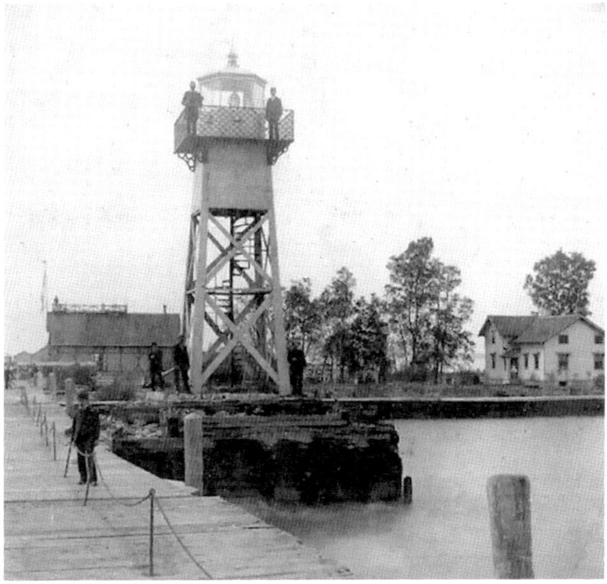

An 1860 photograph of the replacement steel North Pierhead Light after an earlier boating accident. *Courtesy of Erie County Historical Society.*

It took over a year to replace the tower, and this time, a two-story, cast-iron structure equipped with a new sixth-order Fresnel lens was built and placed on a new twenty-eight- by thirty-three-foot pierhead extension. At the same time, a frame dwelling was built on the beach for the keeper. The cost of the tower and pier without the dwelling was $5,250.

During the period of repairs and replacement, a temporary lantern light was hung on an old gallows frame brought in from Pittsburgh. While hanging had gone out of style because of public outrage, it was still legal in the Commonwealth of Pennsylvania, and there were just a few hanging judges sitting on the court benches. Besides, as many people felt, it worked well. As far as a standard for a light at the pier's end, the townspeople and visiting ship captains all felt it was an amusing sight at the channel entrance.

The new light, which commenced operation in 1858, had an iron tower that was twenty-six and a half feet tall. When originally built, the lower portion of the tower was open, showing its spiral staircase, and only the watch room beneath the lantern room was enclosed.

When a new survey was taken in 1864, there was still a depth of twelve feet at the harbor entrance. But the channel was now narrow and crooked and had been driven southward by the sand drifting around the end of the pier. By 1868, the channel was straightened and maintained at a width of one hundred feet. Over the next twelve years, constant work continued on the channel. By 1880, there was a three-hundred-foot-wide

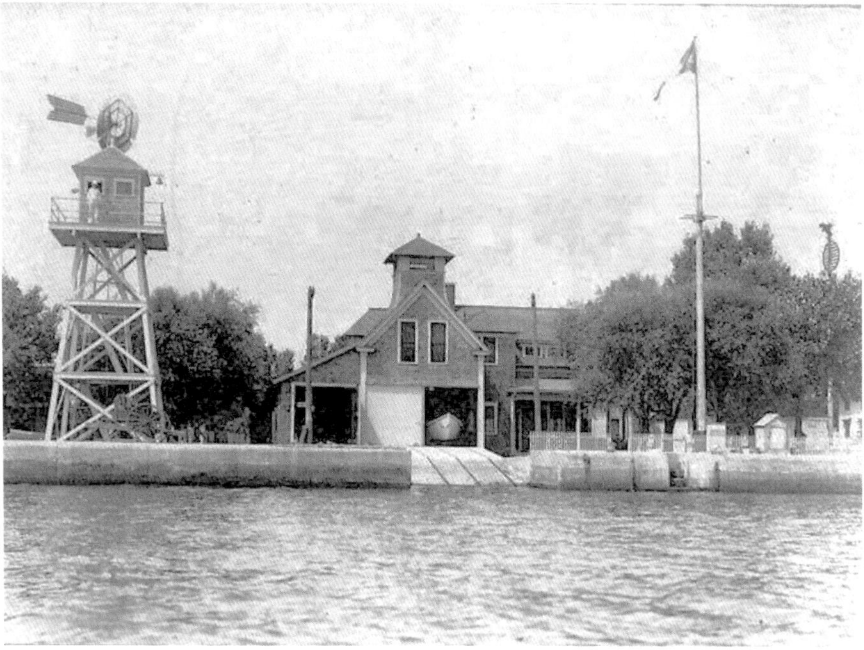

The light and watchtower at the Erie Lafe-Saving Station. *Courtesy of the U.S. Coast Guard.*

channel with a depth not less than sixteen feet from the lake to the deep water in Presque Isle Bay.

There have always been a few lighthouse purists who did not—and a few traditionalists who still do not—classify this well-regarded little light as a true lighthouse. However, it has been officially recognized as such since 1858 when a new cast-iron tower sheathed in steel was erected at the pier's end. However, changes in the Erie harbor, the amount of traffic in and out of it and the continued movement of Presque Isle eastward over the years meant changes in the light. Most people who visit the North Pierhead Light do not realize that it was moved twice more after the 1858 accident and rebuilt at its new location.

As the traffic into the harbor continued to grow, an extension of the channel piers became a necessity. Originally, the light was located at the end of North Pier near where the current Coast Guard station is located. The first home that served the keepers and their families still sits on the grounds of today's Coast Guard station.

In 1872, new octagonal frame towers were erected on the east and west ends of the recently extended pier to serve as range lights for entering the

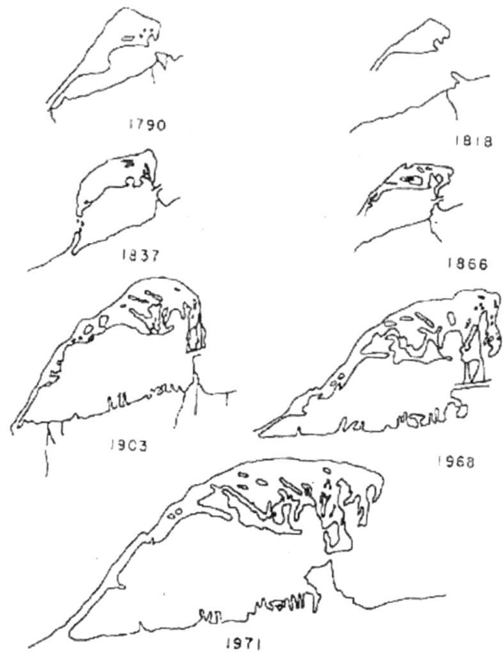

An Army Corps of Engineers representation of the eastward movement of Presque Isle over many years. *Author's collection.*

harbor. At the time, the older, larger iron tower was on its old crib, which was now behind the pier. Then in 1880, a huge fog bell was placed at the eastern end of the pier.

Almost immediately, problems with the bell became apparent. The bell seemed to be inadequate and its sound dull. It was determined, after nearly three years of study, that the density of the freshwater lake air made the bell have a rather doleful "bong" rather than a clear bell sound. The bell also had a directional sound problem that was never figured out. Ship captains told the light keepers that if they were approaching the harbor from the north, the bell could not be heard at all.

Fog has always been a serious problem for mariners throughout the world. Many strange and varied ways to warn ships in the fog were tried over the years. The Boston Light, America's first lighthouse, hosted another first—a special fog signal in the form of cannon. Before this, there were horns blown by the light keepers, shouting into the wind, beating on drums and even a New Jersey lighthouse that handled the fog problem by banging large pots. At the Boston Light, a "great gun" was fired each half-hour during periods of poor visibility to help ships steer out around the shoals of Little Brewster Island. The idea originated with John Hayes, an assistant keeper, at the time called a second keeper, who talked to ship captains and heard them firing their guns in the murky fog. This allowed the ships in the area to know each other's position because the lighthouse was small and could not be seen easily. It did not take long for Hayes to regret his suggestion because soon he found that the gun's concussion upon firing allowed him to get little sleep and brought on serious headaches. The gun was decommissioned and sent to the U.S. Coast Guard Academy in New London, Connecticut. Many cannons were placed at lighthouses over the years until someone in Washington found that the expense of using large amounts of gunpowder to fire the guns cost the federal government over $2,000 a year per gun.

In 1882, when the piers on the Erie channel were widened and lengthened, the light was moved 190 feet to the end of the new pier, and the fog bell was then placed at its base. This base did nothing to help the poor sound of the bell. This iron bell weighed 1,200 pounds. At the same time, the keepers changed from burning whale oil to lard oil. The lard oil, while burning a bit dirtier than whale oil, was more readily available and cost only half as much as the whale oil.

Even while the new, longer piers were under construction, many old salts in town told the government engineers that they were being built incorrectly. They predicted that sand would soon close or clog the ends of the new channel entrance. Less than two months after the work was completed, engineers found the townspeople knew more than they did about the whims of Lake Erie. Sandbars kept filling in at the ends of both new piers. This meant that many years of dredging were needed to remove these sandbars from the entrance areas, at great expense to the federal government.

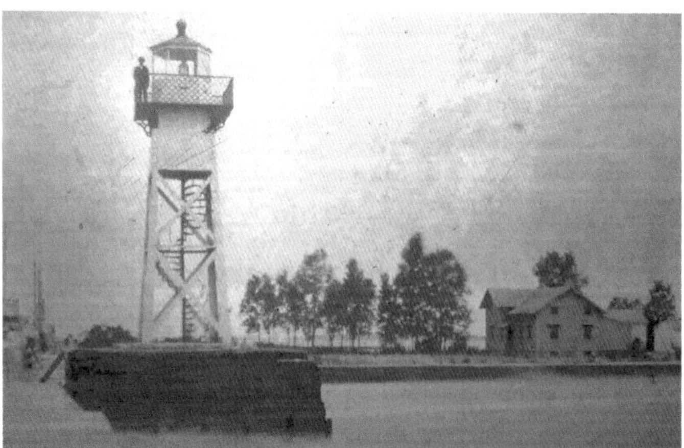

The original North Pier Light. *Courtesy of the Pennsylvania DCNR files.*

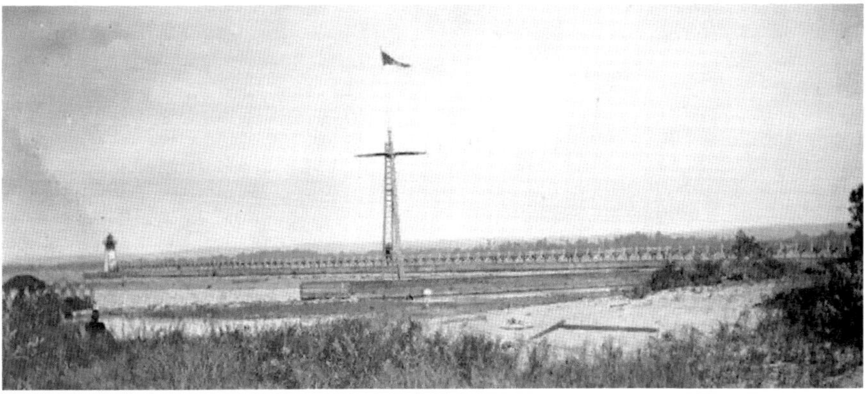

North Pierhead Light with a zip-line. *Courtesy of the Pennsylvania DCNR files.*

In 1883, a few more key changes were made in the North Pierhead Light. One was in the characteristics of the light emitted. The color was changed from a fixed white to a fixed red light. Also added was an elevated walk, 934 feet long, that ran from the iron tower to the keeper's dwelling. The final change was a swap of Fresnel lenses between the North Pierhead Light and the Crossover Island Lighthouse in New York. The North Pier received a fourth-order Fresnel lens, and Crossover Island received a sixth-order lens from the Erie lighthouse.

During 1891, a further extension to North Pier was made that forced the relocation of both the iron tower and the elevated walkway. At that time, a zip-line tower and apparatus were added to the pier. The zip-line was to be used to help take supplies and people to and from the pier. Of course, it became an unauthorized summer fun ride for many Presque Isle visitors.

At about the same time, the Lighthouse Service implemented two new rules. One rule stated that no keepers could be over the age of fifty, and the second rule said keepers were not subject to removal when any change in political officers took place.

Because nearly everyone realized that the fog bell was not working well, work on a new signal started in the spring of 1899. A new building on the northeastern lakefront tip of the ever-changing Presque Isle peninsula was built to house a powerful steam-powered sounding device. Its location was planned for the area that was near what today is Beach 10. The foundation of the building can still be found near the Beach 10 parking lot, right next to the entrance to Pine Tree Trail. It was built roughly a mile north of the North Pierhead Light because the fog bell just was not doing its job, and it had been proven that, in cold water locations, a higher-pitched whistle could easily be heard out on the lake. The location was approximately equidistant between the new Presque Isle Light and the North Pierhead Light and fog bell.

The new steam fog signal station was only operated during times of very low visibility. Its purpose was to warn mariners of the low-lying Presque Isle during extremely foggy, rainy or snowy weather conditions. It was operated by the keepers housed in the Lighthouse Service quarters at the Coast Guard station. These keepers maintained the fog station and made sure it was working at all times. Its ten-inch steam-powered whistle commenced operation in August 1899.

The keepers would travel to the fog station and fire up the steam boilers whenever fog, snow or rain reduced visibility on the lake, which diminished the effectiveness of the lighthouse beacons. These boilers burned almost any available fuel, such as wood, coal or diesel. Coal, as dirty and heavy as it was, was the main fuel used. This fact caused a series of additional problems for the keepers who were assigned to tend the fog station. The large boilers were difficult to get going and very cantankerous once lit, even under the most ideal conditions, and coal was almost always difficult to get started. An even larger problem was that it frequently took practically two hours to build up enough steam to power the whistle. The steam, once generated, would be briefly stored in special storage vessels for use in the whistle.

Still another problem was that fog on the northeastern end of Presque Isle was known to sock in the harbor for days on end. There were rules in place for the fog station, which stated that a keeper must remain on duty at the station at all times when the boiler was running. In 1900, this order necessitated that a second assistant keeper be hired to assist with the fog bell and fog signal station. When this additional keeper was hired, a new two-family residence was built, and the lighthouse keeper and first assistant moved into it. The new keeper moved into the former residence. In the summer of 2015, the new commander of the U.S. Coast Guard Station at Presque Isle supervised the removal of these buildings from the base. Both were listed on the National Historic Register.

The keepers serviced the fog whistle on a regular schedule, and keeping a sufficient supply of fuel for the boiler was a large part of their duties. Once the boilers had built up steam, it would be released through a ten-inch whistle at strictly prescribed time intervals. This indicated to sailors where they were on the lake. Almost all ship captains on the lake had charts aboard their ships indicating that five seconds of sound followed by twenty-five seconds

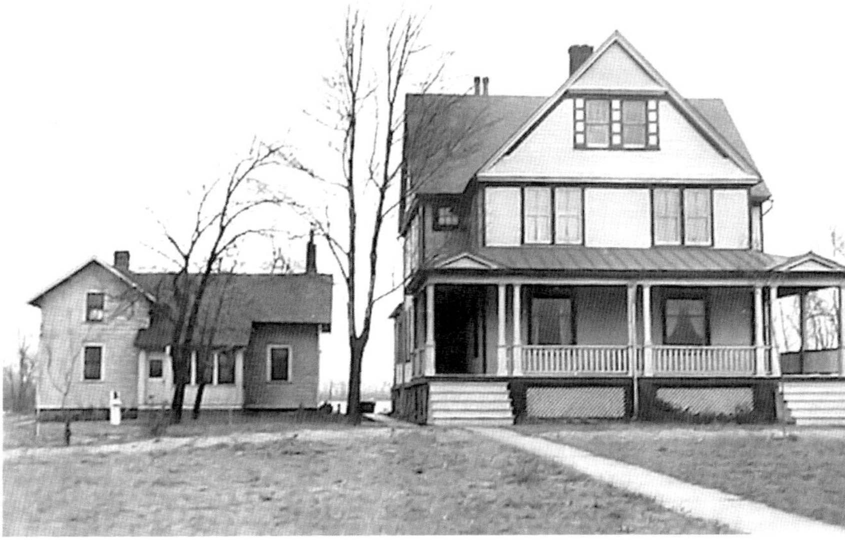

Two keepers' residences built at the U.S. Coast Guard Station in Erie. *Courtesy of the U.S. Coast Guard.*

of silence meant they were approaching Presque Isle. This steam whistle, in combination with the North Pier Fog Bell that rang every ten seconds, was easily distinguished by vessels on the water, by both sound type and interval. This process was, of course, very hard work for the keepers, who still had their lighthouse duties at the same time.

Within twenty years, with the migration of Presque Isle nearly six hundred feet more to the northeast, the original steam fog whistle was now located well inland, causing it to lose much of its effectiveness. Also, new technology allowed for automatic signals to be used, reducing the need for keepers to travel to the fog whistle. In 1924, a new electric signal was built to replace the steam whistle.

This new signal tower and signal were built on the now northeasternmost tip of Presque Isle. This was some 625 feet from the old steam fog station. In the end, this signal was also taken out of service in 1957. Again, the eastward migration of Presque Isle was a key reason. This new tower was now over one-third of a mile inland. The four concrete footers for this tower base remain today at the edge of the eastern parking lot of Beach 10.

In addition to the fog bell and the steam fog whistle, keepers needed to service all functions assigned to the North Pierhead Light. This included keeping the areas around their living quarters at the Life-Saving Service

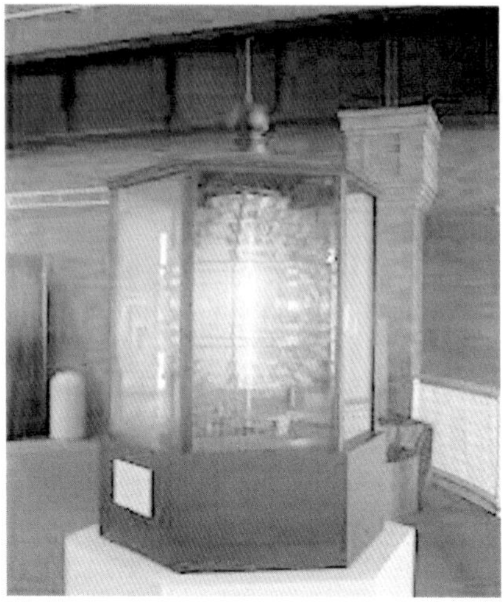

A photograph of the Fresnel lens that was once used in the North Pierhead Light. *Author's collection.*

headquarters neat and clean. About 1900, the fog bell was removed from the base of the iron tower and placed in an open framework structure at the end of the pier. This framework came from the lighthouse in Dunkirk, New York. However, after just five years, it was soon found no longer to be practical to operate the bell, and it was removed from the pier.

In the summer of 1924, the lights on the pier were electrified. An underwater cable was run from the city to Presque Isle in the spring of that year. Shortly after, a new fog signal, in the form of a loud and deep-sounding horn, was housed within the tower. Remote control could operate this signal from the shore-based powerhouse, and life became much easier for the keepers of this light.

The next and last move of the lighthouse took place in 1940 when again the pier was extended, and the light moved to its eastern end. This extension of the pier changed the general direction of the pier and slanted it in a more northeasterly direction. This new extension added another 509 feet to the length of North Pier and stopped the sandbar problem almost immediately. Normal storm sand movement continued, and even now, some dredging is periodically needed to keep the channel at a fairly even depth.

Once the light was moved, the Lighthouse Service boxed in the tower with heavy steel plating and painted its distinctive large black and white stripes. The design of the lighthouse and its steel cover is unique because it is the only surviving example of the square and pyramidal–style lighthouse tower left in the United States. One other unique fact about this little lighthouse is that the plating and additional bracing needed to enclose the lighthouse were made in France and shipped to Erie for assembly. The last change in the light was in 1995, when the light began to be powered by solar panels, and the Coast Guard changed the light's fixed red light to a flashing red light and donated the fourth-order Fresnel lens to the Erie Maritime Museum.

Today, the North Pier Light is a significant tourist attraction. It draws visitors from all over Canada and the United States. They come to see the

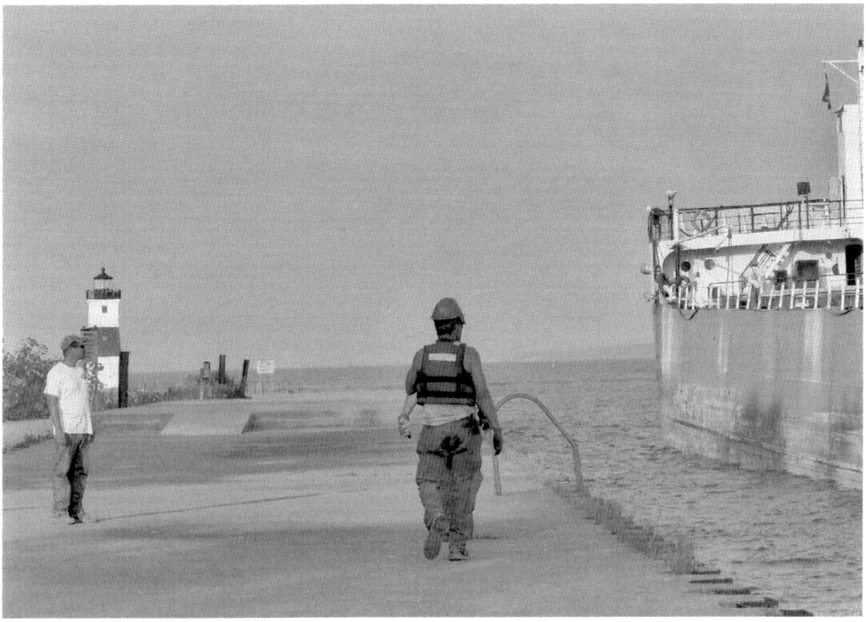

The crew of a lake freighter docking the ship at North Pier. *Author's collection.*

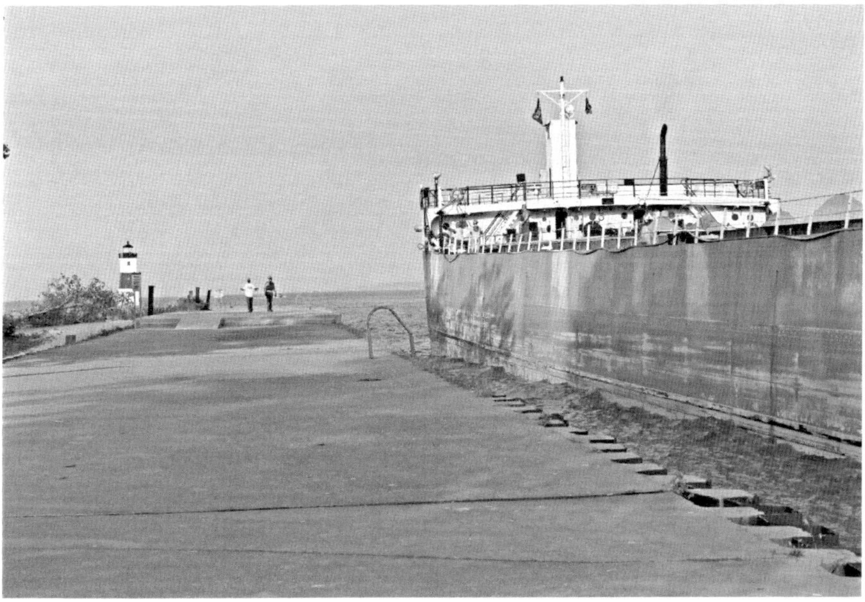

An 890-foot-long lake freighter docking at North Pier to discharge sand for erosion control on Presque Isle State Park. The North Pierhead Light is in the background. *Author's collection.*

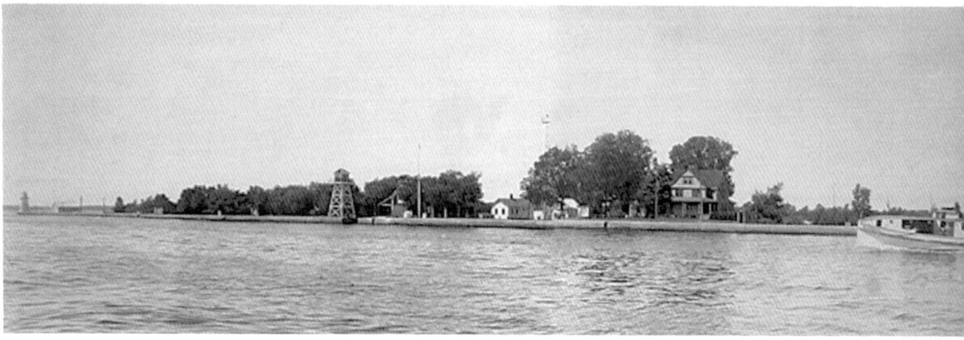

Top: Fishing boats moving into Harbor Channel with North Pierhead Light in background, 1924. *Author's collection.*

Above: The North Pierhead Light early on a summer morning. *Author's collection.*

Opposite: A Sunday sailboat race going past the North Pierhead Light early in the morning. *Courtesy of Jerry Skrypzak.*

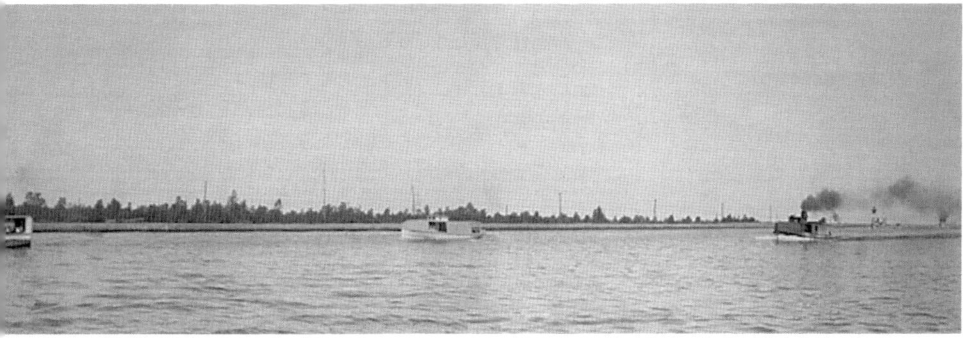

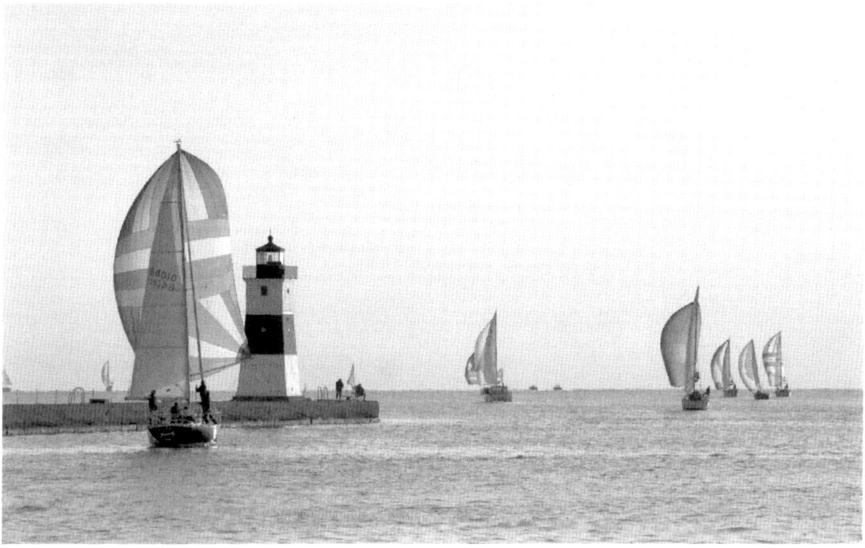

little lighthouse but stay quite a while to watch the immense boat and ship traffic passing through the Erie harbor entrance. Also, each and every day will find fishermen and their families lining both sides of the channel to wet their fishing lines. This is a wonderful spot to fish with its thirty- to forty-foot-deep waters and at least twenty species of large and small fish waiting to take a fisherman's bait. Summer days find moms, dads and kids lining the piers and filling their buckets with fish of all sorts.

Early mornings are unique at the lighthouse because of its location near the eastern end of Presque Isle. Erie has forever been renowned for its sunrises and sunsets, so from 5:15 a.m. to 7:00 a.m., depending on the time of year, you will find many photographers at their favorite spots shooting the sun as it slides up over the eastern horizon. You can almost count on the North Pierhead Light being included in 80 percent of all pictures.

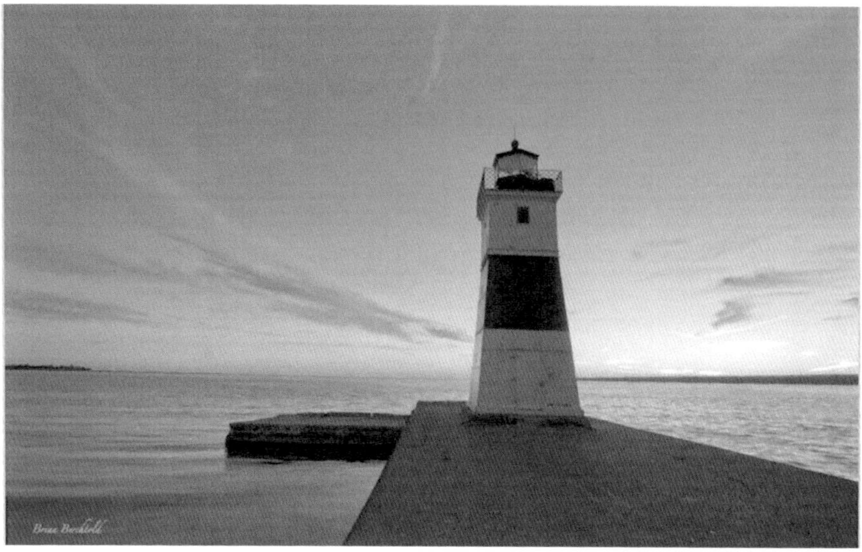

Sunrise over North Pierhead Light, 2012. *Author's collection.*

The light itself may be small, yet year after year, it continues to perform its all-important functions as an aid to navigation to ships approaching the harbor of Erie and to be an amazing attraction to the people who visit Presque Isle.

"North Pierhead Light"

Born in 1800 and 28,
To lead sailors to Erie's channel gate.
Many nights the lake seems calm as glass,
When out of the dark,
A thunderstorm comes to pass.
As winds let out an awesome cry,
Bolts of lightning torment the sky.

Rounding the point, sails tattered and torn,
North Pierhead Light shines through the storm.
Her unwavering light will surely hold the key,
To a safe return from the stormy and troubled lake.
If nature's evening storms bring you pain,
Always remember.
Rainbows follow the rain.
—Eugene H. Ware

6

NAMES FROM THE PAST

THE LIGHTHOUSE ESTABLISHMENT, THE LIFE-SAVING SERVICE AND THE REVENUE CUTTER SERVICE

During this country's colonial period, which is considered by many experts to be before 1780, each of the then functioning colonial governments built, owned and operated all lighthouses along its own shorelines. It was a haphazard patchwork of aids to navigation, as each colony set its own rules and regulations for its lights. By 1789, there were twelve lighthouses in operation by the colonies. In addition, there were new lights being built each year, as local people lobbied their elected representatives for them.

On August 7, 1789, President George Washington signed the ninth act of the first U.S. Congress, which stipulated that the new states turn over their lighthouses, both those under construction and existing, to the central government. It created what was known as the U.S. Lighthouse Establishment. Under this act, all aids to navigation became the responsibility of the secretary of the treasury. At that time, the secretary was Alexander Hamilton.

From the very beginning, both Hamilton and Washington were actively involved with all decisions about the lighthouses. In 1792, Hamilton turned the administration of lighthouses over to the commissioner of revenue until Albert Gallatin became the secretary of the treasury. He controlled the lighthouses for eight years, and when he left the office, the responsibility for the lighthouses went back to the commissioner of revenue. Finally, in 1820, that office was abolished, and the fifth auditor of the treasury, Stephen Pleasonton, was assigned the lighthouse responsibilities.

The first public works project in the United States was the building of the Cape Henry Lighthouse in 1792. This lighthouse was built on Bay Island, which is just north of Virginia Beach, on the Chesapeake Bay. President George Washington took a very personal interest in this light and ended up approving each and every aspect of its construction. Presidents Adams and Jefferson also kept a close watch and sometimes also took control of all lighthouse operations and construction during their administrations. This initial high level of involvement by Washington, Adams, Jefferson and Hamilton was tied directly to the new country's need for active trading and its desire to be able to compete with other world powers.

From 1820 to 1852, Steven Pleasonton held his job as head of the Lighthouse Establishment. However, beginning in 1847, the responsibility for construction of six lighthouses was granted to the Army Corps of Engineers, and Pleasonton's reign of control came to an end. In 1852, he was removed from his position. During August of that year, the U.S. Lighthouse Establishment became the U.S. Lighthouse Board, largely due to the huge number of complaints about the condition of U.S. lighthouses.

Under the direction of the Lighthouse Board, the country was divided into eight districts, including two for the Great Lakes. An inspector was appointed for each district. In all cases, the first inspector was a naval officer with many years' experience. That inspector handled overall construction, maintenance and purchasing within his district. These officers found the general conditions of the lights to range from good to terrible. Their reports told of much faulty construction and maintenance and inadequate lighting systems, plus many poorly placed lighthouses.

The Lighthouse Board itself had nine members and was composed mainly of experienced naval and army engineering officers. The results of this change were amazing. Over the next thirty years, the very nature of how lighthouses were built and maintained changed dramatically. It soon became apparent that the number of districts needed to be increased, so in 1886, the number was expanded to sixteen. Over the next thirty years, the Lighthouse Board became the Bureau of Lighthouses, and the number of districts was again increased. This increase took the districts now to nineteen. At the same time, the new bureau introduced the reinforced concrete lighthouse tower. The new bureau was eventually assigned to the Department of Commerce.

When the U.S. Lighthouse Board changed to the Bureau of Lighthouses, there were 11,713 aids to navigation of all types in this country. Over its fifty-eight-year lifespan, the U.S. Lighthouse Board accomplished all it had been asked to do and then passed on to its successor an exceptionally well-run agency with a long history of success.

While all this was going on, many citizens and governmental bodies began to realize that the Great Lakes provided a natural waterway for the transportation of goods and people to and from the rich American heartland. During the 1800s and early 1900s, the lakes practically acted like a superhighway to the western reaches of the country. The lakes have continually formed the most important inland waterway in North America. As early pioneers found during their push westward, these vast lakes were not like most of the other lakes in the world. These were lakes that could generate waves twenty feet in height or higher and did so without warning, and this could occur quite quickly. If you look at the statistics on the Great Lakes, you will find that they are truly a huge combined body of water containing fully 22 percent of the world's fresh water. These lakes also encompass a little over 95,500 square miles. Each of the lakes has its own unique temperament and characteristics depending on location, depth or, in the case of Lake Erie and Lake Ontario, orientation to the prevailing weather patterns. This causes storms to be quite severe and come roaring down the lake with a vengeance. Lake Erie is more like a river than a large lake, with a constant west-to-east current due to its shallowness and the fact that Niagara Falls and its associated Niagara River drain the lake at a rapid rate.

Back in the 1800s, most sailors were saltwater mariners who, when transitioning to the Great Lakes, would often ask locals what danger there could be from just a lake. They soon learned that there could be great and perilous danger lurking on the lakes. There was as much peril for ships on the Great Lakes as there was for ships on the oceans of the world.

The establishment of the Life-Saving Service traces its beginning to the slow and politically rocky road of legislative action in the halls and cloakrooms of Congress. In fact, the very first federal appropriation that would eventually lead to the formation of the Life-Saving Service was passed in 1847. The simple reasoning behind this law was to provide funds for rendering assistance from the shore to victims of a shipwreck. The allocation was very small and, unfortunately, was not actually used as directed. The Massachusetts Humane Society, which already maintained sixteen boathouses, used the money to build small shoreline huts along the shores of the Commonwealth of Massachusetts. They were built along exposed and isolated areas of the coast where mariners might need shelter after a shipwreck.

On August 14, 1848, the federal Life-Saving Service, not yet officially named or authorized by Congress, effectively began to function. It was on that day, in an amendment to an important lighthouse bill, that Representative William Newell added language that would provide $10,000 to purchase surfboats, rockets and other necessary equipment to provide for the preservation of life and property from shipwrecks off the coast of New Jersey. This appropriation allowed the Treasury Department to build eight small lifeboat stations and furnish them. Once done, a full complement of rescue equipment plus a galvanized iron surfboat were provided for each lifeboat station. With this, the congressional gridlock had been cleared. In March of the following year, Congress approved an additional $20,000, and sixteen more lifeboat stations were built along the Atlantic coast. In the following years, the Life-Saving Service quickly expanded, and it became an agency of the federal government.

As mentioned in the last chapter, during this same time, the government bodies were adding new and needed lighthouses all across the Great Lakes and along the Atlantic and Gulf coasts. In 1848, the Erie North Channel Tower Light displayed its simple lantern light at the harbor entrance for the first time. At that time, the Presque Isle Light had been operational for over thirty years.

Closely related to the Life-Saving Service, and eventually merging with it to form the U.S. Coast Guard, was the United States Revenue Cutter Service, established originally as the Revenue Marine. Authorized and named by Secretary of the Treasury Alexander Hamilton, this agency was established in 1790 to serve as a maritime law enforcement agency. By the 1820s, it had cutters touring the Great Lakes while enforcing revenue laws and assisting ships in distress. It also took on the responsibilities of collecting customs duties whenever asked to help by local jurisdictions. Until it finally merged with the Life-Saving Service in 1915, the agency was under the jurisdiction of the Treasury Department, so the collection of duties became a naturally added duty for the Revenue Cutter Service. In 1939, the final change to the Lighthouse Bureau was its merger with the Revenue Cutter Service into the U.S. Coast Guard, where it remains today. Finally, the spin-the-bottle nature of the lighthouse administration came to an end. With this merger, the combined agencies became known officially as the United States Coast Guard.

As years passed, the Coast Guard grew and was assigned many additional duties. On July 1, 1939, one of these responsibilities became maintaining the country's aids to navigation, including all lighthouses. Before this, the United States Lighthouse Service was handling this duty. The Lighthouse Service traces its roots back to 1716, with the establishment of a lighthouse on Little

Brewster Island (as related in the preface). Today's Coast Guard began as the United States Life-Saving Service, the agency that was born out of safety and humanitarian efforts and of both private and governmental concerns. Its goal was to save the lives of shipwrecked mariners and passengers.

With the Coast Guard having control and responsibility for safety on the lakes and the lighthouses, it is easy to see why the Erie Coast Guard and the Erie lighthouses on Presque Isle were always strongly bound together in the past. Currently, of the three Erie lighthouses, only the Erie Land Lighthouse, which today functions as a historical museum, has never been connected to the Coast Guard. The Coast Guard today has total authority over the actual functioning of the aid to navigation portion of the two operational lighthouses on Presque Isle.

David P. Dobbins, son of Daniel P. Dobbins, was instrumental in leading the ongoing efforts to establish a lifesaving station in Erie. However, he could never get funds approved to accomplish this task. Many legislators believed the idea was worthy, but when it came to providing funding, they all kept silent. It was not until 1870, when a series of shipwrecks with many deaths occurred in the Erie area, that the citizens of Erie plus the state and local governments really began working to convince Congress to approve a lifesaving station for Erie. The lifesaving station on Presque Isle was established by an act of Congress in 1876. Prior to this, Dobbins was appointed a superintendent of the Ninth District of the Life-Saving Service, which comprised the American shores of Lake Erie and Ontario and a portion of the Ohio River. His influence in Washington was growing.

A Colonel Berriman came to Erie and Presque Isle in October 1874 to select a site for the new station. He came to town on the USRC *Sherman*. Because a majority of the marine disasters occurred near the point of Presque Isle, a site on its north shore was selected. The site was nearly three miles from the new Presque Isle Light Station, commonly known at the time as the "Flash Light." The full history of this lighthouse will be covered in Chapter 7. In May 1876, a contract was awarded to Mr. Schwartz, a Buffalo contractor, to build the new lifesaving station on Presque Isle. The awarding of the contract angered many of the townspeople, who believed it should have gone to an Erie-based contractor who knew the problems with the station's planned location. Having experienced a similar situation at the Land Lighthouse and the Milwaukee brick problems, many citizens lost faith and trust in everyone associated with the federal government or its agencies.

The citizens' concerns turned out to be right. Both Colonel Berriman and the contractor were not familiar with the storm conditions in this area of Lake Erie, and serious problems began to develop immediately. Berriman located the station at what was one of the worst locations possible on Presque Isle for such a facility. Many townspeople told Berriman and Schwartz that the location would never work; however, they would not change their minds about the site. One of Berriman's prime reasons for choosing this location was that it was near the mid-point between the North Pierhead Light and the new Presque Isle Light Station.

Almost immediately after Berriman left Erie, the brig *Wacoma* brought the material necessary to build the station to Presque Isle. Under orders from Berriman, this material was dropped off and stored on the nearby Presque Isle Light Station pier. This was, yet again, not a good decision. The very next day, a massive gale slammed in off the lake from the west, and a large portion of the material was swept away and never recovered. This should have caused Berriman to reconsider the location, but he did not.

The station, however, was completed before the end of the summer, and by September, a new Hingston Surfboat was delivered for use at the new facility. Initially, a seven-man crew was assigned to the station. Clark Jones was appointed captain of the crew. The backbone and soul of the Life-Saving Service were these surfmen. They would typically stand duty or be on call eighty-four hours a week. Many times, the surfmen were chosen from the local community because it was felt that they might have had valuable experience with the waves and weather conditions. The surfmen handled search and rescue planning, operations and equipment. They were also expected to operate in the most extreme weather conditions. These men still exist in the Coast Guard to this day. At that time, all lifesaving stations on Lake Erie and most of the Great Lakes were kept fully operational only during the bad weather months of September, October and November.

When the Life-Saving Service opened, the stations were organized as a separate agency of the Department of the Treasury. As the man in charge of the lifesaving station in Erie, William Clark was named the keeper in 1877. He served until his death by drowning in 1891. After being born in Denmark, Clark, who went to sea at the age of fifteen, moved to Erie and sailed the Great Lakes for nearly six more years before taking the position of keeper at the new station. He had many years of maritime experience and had handled both men and boats in challenging situations. It was the habit of the Coast Guard to retain keepers for many years in the same or very similar areas so that they would gain valuable experience with the weather and wave conditions of their bases. The first station's location on the lakeside, where most of the wrecks and storm troubles occurred, presented many future problems to the surfboat crews.

This location proved to be both dangerous and impracticable much of the time due to the pounding waves of the lake that were common at the point of Presque Isle. Soon after the station opened, a three-masted schooner became stranded south of the channel and east of the breakwall in a strong northeastern gale. During the storm, the schooner's only lifeboats were washed away. The surfmen at the new lifesaving station were totally unsuccessful after many attempts to launch the station's boat in the thundering ten- to fourteen-foot waves coming off Lake Erie. As a last resort, Captain Clark Jones had the boat mounted on a wagon and drawn by volunteers across the peninsula to the harbor channel entrance. The boat was launched there and began a long and dangerous trip out to the schooner in the black of night. It left with only a small lantern lashed to its front to provide the sailors on the schooner a point of reference to watch for as the surfmen approached.

As the night progressed, the gale continued at full force. The waves were huge, and the wind kept howling. Of course, word quickly spread all through the town about the impending disaster, and throngs of Erie citizens gathered on the shore. Most watchers felt they would witness the complete destruction of the schooner with the possible total loss of all members of the crew. The only thing the people watching could see was the little lantern of the surfboat rise, fall and disappear into the inky darkness of the gale. Finally, the light disappeared entirely. After what seemed like hours, a light again appeared out of the black. To observers, it seemed to be coming toward them. Finally, the surfboat with the rescued crew aboard hauled up safely alongside the channel pier.

The dreadful experience of that night's storm was a clear indication that the station would need to be relocated if it were to accomplish its mission. Everyone saw that it was impossible for lifeboats to be launched from the station's lakeside location in foul weather. It only took until early in 1878 to receive the orders from the chief lighthouse inspector in Washington to move the station to its current location on the harbor channel. This was during the time that the harbor and the expansion and development of the city as a major lake port became Erie's primary focus. The moving of the station would significantly contribute to the efforts of the city to reinforce the safety of Erie's harbor operations.

Captain David P. Dobbins, now superintendent of all lifesaving stations, met in Erie with Commander W.R. Bridgeman of the United States Navy,

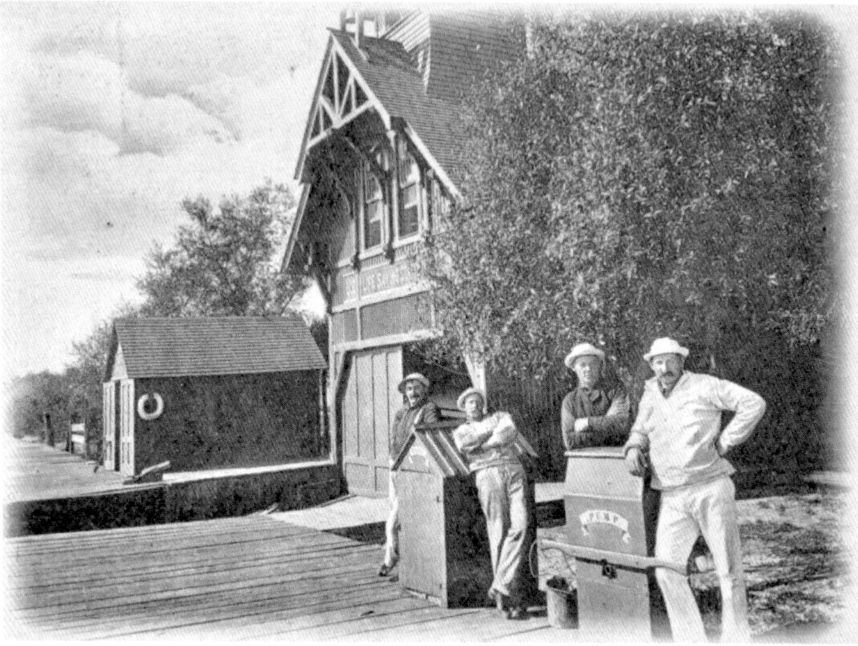

A group of surfmen at the lifesaving station in Erie, 1900. *Courtesy of the Pennsylvania DCNR files.*

who was also the lighthouse inspector of the Tenth District, during February 1878.Their mission was to select the new site for the station. They had known before they met that it must be located somewhere along the harbor channel on what was known at the time as that lighthouse's property. They also made arrangements to award a contract to move the existing building and equipment from its lakeside location by wagons and trucks. This work took only six weeks to complete, and local contractors did the work.

David P. Dobbins was also known for designing and testing a new form of pulling lifeboat in 1878. It was a self-righting and self-bailing boat. It was widely used in the Great Lakes and Atlantic coastal areas. Its dimensions varied somewhat depending on the builder and its intended operating station assignment. Its length could vary from twenty-four to thirty-two feet and its weight from 2,000 to 8,400 pounds. It was usually built from pine or cedar planking over an oak frame with copper fasteners. Dobbins's design was lighter, more maneuverable and cost less than half of all other lifeboats available at the time.

7

PRESQUE ISLE LIGHT STATION

When proposed, it sounded quite simple: build a better-located new lighthouse on Presque Isle to make it safer to sail Lake Erie and to make entry into the Erie harbor easier for mariners. Congress had approved a budget, plans were drawn, a specific location on Presque Isle was chosen and bid information was sent to contractors.

When it was announced that a new lighthouse on the peninsula was being planned, many citizens thought it was a crazy idea. Wasn't the old Presque Isle Light east of Erie still functioning? Did the planners realize that there were no roads on Presque Isle? What about when the peninsula was cut off from the mainland and became an island? How would construction workers, tools and material get to the site of the lighthouse? Once built, how would the lighthouse keeper and his family get supplies? The townspeople thought that attempting to build a lighthouse out on Presque Isle would cause serious problems.

They had some extremely good reasons to believe this. During this period, the peninsula had become an island many times, and it was always under threat to do so again. Presque Isle was covered with wild old growth and new timber from the mainland to the eastern tip. Many were worried that fires, which were common on Presque Isle, would increase due to the lighthouse. Only when Lake Erie breached into the bay and cleared the western end of Presque Isle of timber did open areas appear. The whole landmass of Presque Isle was a series of swamps, ponds and lagoons that made walking on the peninsula very difficult if not impossible. Most people in early Erie

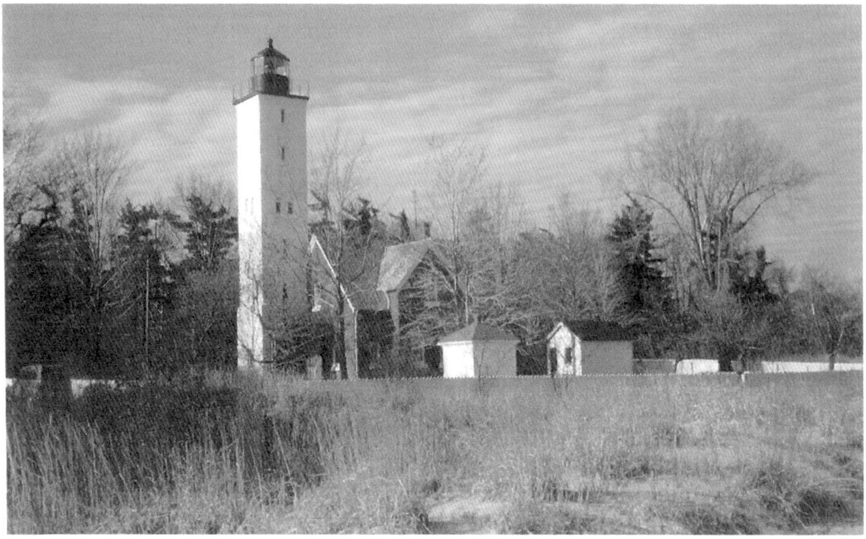

Presque Isle Light Station with white fence, 1952. *Author's collection.*

thought Presque Isle "too wild" to be of any use except for picnicking and fishing around the bay front edges. Most residents had never ventured to the lake side of Presque Isle because they felt it was too dangerous.

The townspeople were right about the old Presque Isle Light, as it was still working fine at that time. Not being mariners, they did not recognize that only ships coming from the northeast could see the lighthouse as they approached the Erie harbor. The migration of Presque Isle to the east nearly completely blocked line-of-sight from the west and northwest. This fact made the old lighthouse useless to most ships approaching the Erie harbor. After much discussion, they finally began to accept the idea of a new lighthouse.

Congress authorized $10,000 to build the lighthouse on Presque Isle. When the project went out to bid, the Lighthouse Board received many replies. However, the lowest bid was $15,400 and the highest was $28,900, and none of them included transportation of material and supplies to the site. This was to be part of the requirements of bidding. That meant that there were no qualified bids. Twelve weeks later, the government changed the design and bidding procedures slightly. It also changed some delivery requirements and terms and decided to raise the budget to $15,000 so the project could get started.

By this time, everyone was convinced that the new light was needed to warn mariners of the seven-mile-long peninsula jutting out into Lake Erie on what was an otherwise straight coastline. However, when the second round of bids went out, they were again too high. More design changes were then made to keep the light's construction within the allocated budget. For example, the main construction material was changed from limestone to the functional but cheaper brick. The basic floor plan of the lighthouse never changed. Now a qualified bid was received and accepted, so construction could finally begin. The lighthouse construction was initiated on September 2, 1872, six months after the planned starting date.

As stated, the site was very isolated and totally undeveloped at the time. The only direct approach by water was considered highly dangerous due to the total unpredictability of the lake. Contractors soon found that no insurance company was willing to bond the project due to what they considered a very high probability of serious problems during construction. Very early in the project, the contractors found that the insurance companies were right. A scow with six thousand bricks was lost as it was trying to deliver them to the site. Many small boats trying to deliver people, tools and material to the lighthouse site also were damaged, overturned or sunk during the early stages of construction. The contractors realized that a new way was needed to bring workers, tools and supplies to the site.

Ultimately, in the late fall of 1872, after a number of accidents and the sinking of six supply boats in Lake Erie, many workmen opted to row to their job sites daily from the city and land at a very rough spot on Misery Bay. They then walked to the lighthouse site on the lake side using what was just a crude winding path they had carved through the swamps. At the same time, some of the supplies and material also began to arrive via this route from Misery Bay. After landing at Misery Bay, the material and tools were hand-loaded onto wagons. The workmen, using horses and mules, would then haul the supplies and material along this two-mile swampy path. This path was always wet and full of mud and ruts.

Still, even with the danger involved, a good deal of the material continued to be delivered by boat to the lakeside site. Although the construction was going well, receiving the right material—and enough of it—was a major problem that beleaguered the project during the fall construction season. The project was closed down on December 8, 1872, for the winter season. This was due to early season gales and storms coming in off Lake Erie. Even with the serious problems of supply, the house and tower had been completed up to the top of the first-story windows. Most of the roof beams were already cut and ready to be put into place as soon as the residence's walls were completed in the spring. For protection from the winter storms,

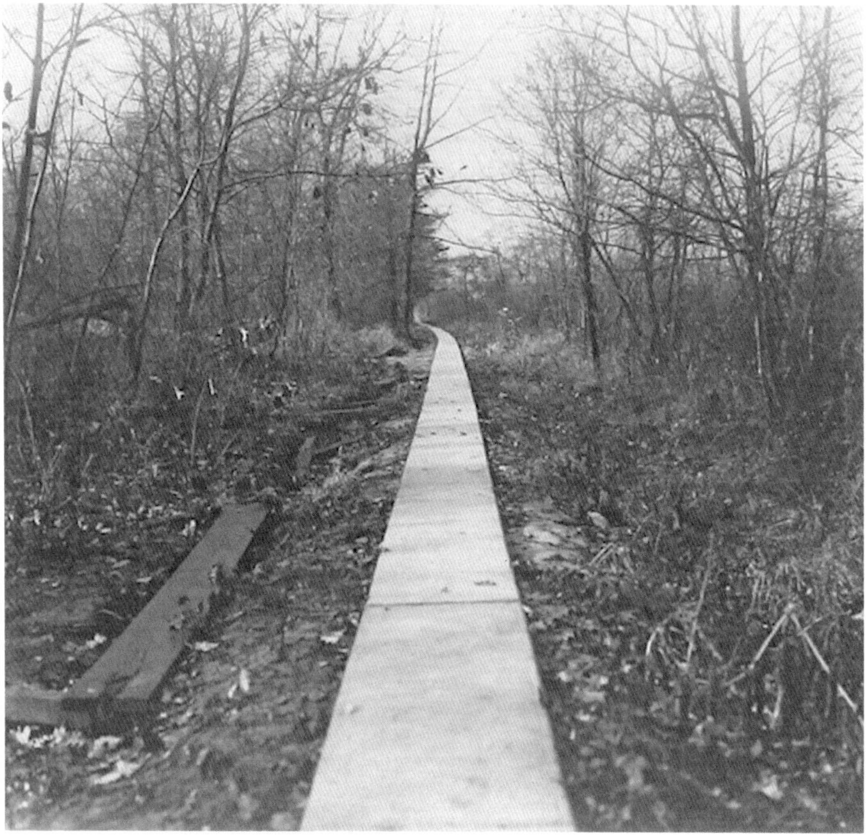

The sidewalk path from Presque Isle Light Station to the boathouse on Misery Bay. *Courtesy of the Pennsylvania DCNR files.*

workers covered the area and materials with canvas or boarded them up. These actions totally closed down the project. The contractor hired a watchman to protect the site over the winter. Unfortunately, the watchman walked off the job and quit after only forty days due to the appalling weather and the complete boredom of being isolated on Presque Isle.

As soon as ice was off the bay, which was in early March that year, crews set about modifying a better 1.5-mile crude, narrow but now straight pathway to connect the new lighthouse with Misery Bay. At first, this pathway was just a sandy path built through the swampy interior. As spring went on, wooden boards were added to make travel easier by bridging the very wet and muddy portions that were always being threatened by the changing water levels of Lake Erie. Because Presque Isle is a sand spit, all the water in the swamps, lagoons and ponds tends to rise and fall in direct proportion to whatever happens to water levels on the lake. So when the lake is high, whole new areas are likely to flood or get extremely wet. The water table under Presque Isle is down less than two feet below ground level in most areas.

Before the roads were built on Presque Isle, which was over fifty years later, this pathway that cut right across the park was the only access from the lighthouse to the mainland. In 1880, it was fully covered with wooden boards to make walking easier. At the time, it was called the "Old Plank Walk." It was rebuilt two more times, in 1895 and 1906, before being paved in 1925 with concrete. Even after a road was opened, many of the light keepers still used this way to town because it saved them one and a half hours of travel time instead of using the road. As part of creating the interior path, work was started and completed on a boathouse on Misery Bay for storage of the light keeper's rowboat that he would use to go into town.

Since it was felt that the lighthouse needed to be completed as soon as possible, work was restarted on April 16, 1873, even though the weather that spring was far from ideal. The path from Misery Bay was not yet fully complete when work was to start, so the work crews were forced to use horses and mules to help carry material over the partially done sections of the path, causing increased delays in construction.

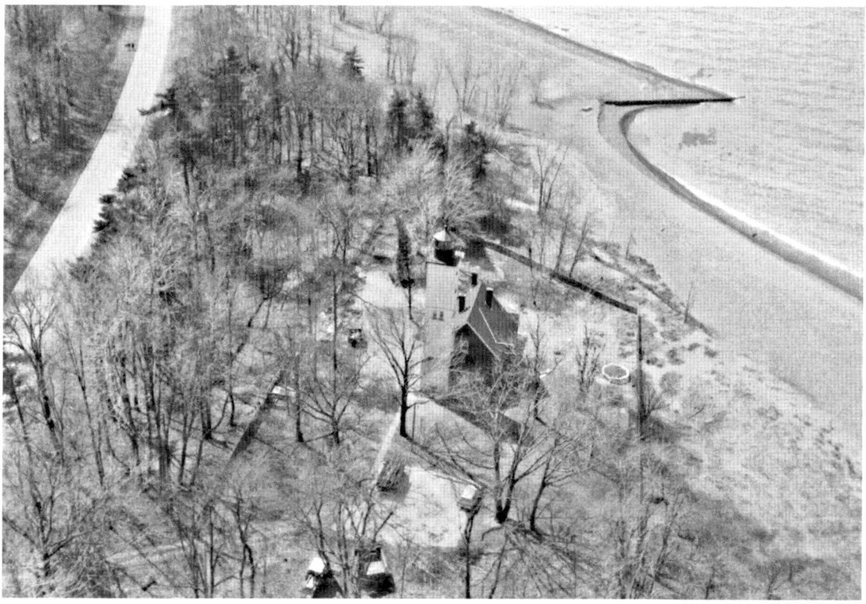

An aerial view of the Presque Isle Light Station showing beach erosion to the west of the light. *Courtesy of Pennsylvania DCNR files.*

Work on the tower became the key to moving the project forward, so extra workmen were added early that spring to finish work on the forty-foot brick structure. The tower was square on the outside and round on the inside. It was five courses of brick thick to protect it from the fierce fall, winter and spring storms that had a habit of ravishing the Presque Isle shoreline. The tower also supported an iron spiral staircase, forged in Pittsburgh and barged to Erie on the Erie Extension Canal. That staircase is still in use today.

The construction crews were doing a masterful job, and because of this, the contractor was able to inform the Lighthouse Service that on April 30, 1873, the tower was ready for the installation of the lantern. By May 31, the lantern was in place, and only the plastering and painting within the tower was left to be finished in compliance with the lighthouse contract.

The lantern room is the key to a lighthouse. It is that portion of the top of a lighthouse tower that encloses the lens. In this case, it was constructed by a manufacturer and transported in sections to the lighthouse. It was then

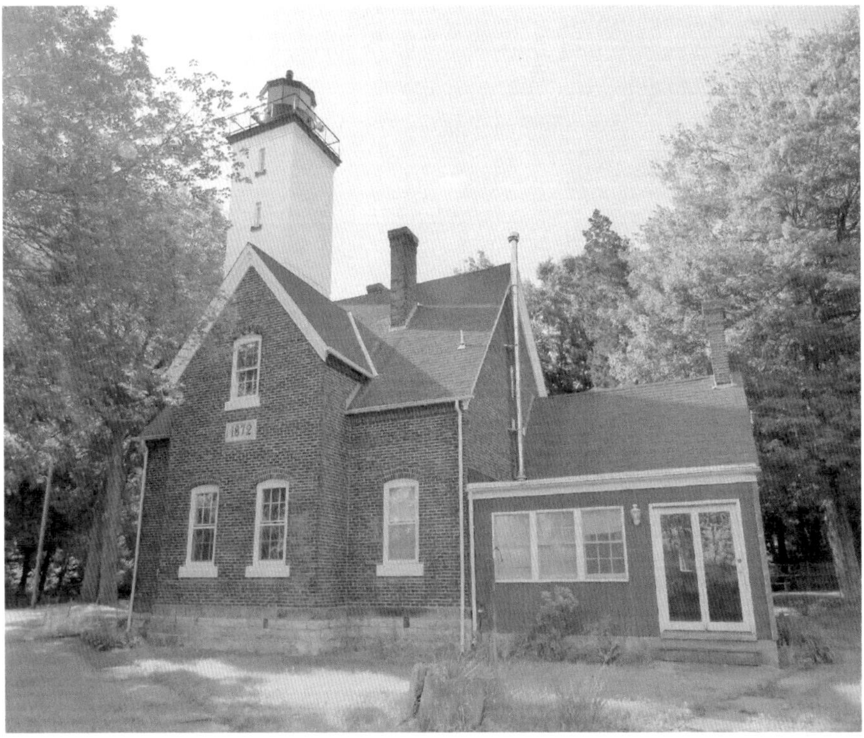

A spring 2014 photograph of the Presque Isle Light Station after the removal of trees that were blocking the light's effectiveness. *Author's collection.*

assembled on top of the tower. The lantern room is made up of three parts: the service room; the optics area; and the dome and ventilator ball.

One of the most important jobs of a light keeper was to know all about the ventilator ball. In the evening, the keeper would climb to the lantern room and check the wind direction and speed. He would then adjust the vents to allow correct draft into the lantern room. He would need to adjust the ventilator each day. The wind passing through the ball vent would create a certain amount of a vacuum that would pull the draft up to the top of the lantern room. This draft and vacuum also kept the interior glass of the room clear of fog and sucked the fumes from the oil-burning lamp or lamps up the vent tube to the ball and out of the lighthouse. This made the lantern burn better and was a safety measure for the keeper and his family.

The circle within a square design of the interior of the tower allowed for a hidden chain and weight-timing mechanism, much like an old-fashioned weight-and-pendulum-style clock. Its purpose was to provide the power for a series of short pieces of apparatus that would automatically turn and manipulate the light at timed intervals. Those timing weights can still be seen in the corners of the lighthouse's tower and can be accessed through small wooden doors. It was part of the keeper's job to keep the weights pulled up to the top of the tower throughout the night. Eventually, this weight system was converted to an intricate electrical arrangement of batteries, generators and power lines. That system is still in use. Only once did it totally break down. That happened while Frank Huntington was the keeper. His solution was to sit next to the Fresnel lens and turn it by hand. It took three days for the system to be fixed, and Huntington continued his long nightly duties for those three nights.

In a strange twist, when the United States Lighthouse Service merged with the Coast Guard, Huntington, who was the keeper of the Presque Isle Light Station at that time, immediately became a member of the Coast Guard. This was due to how the legislation was worded. At the same time, the responsibility for the operation of the Presque Isle Light Station and the North Pierhead Light was assumed by the Ninth Coast Guard District, which was headquartered in Cleveland, Ohio.

The tower was designed to hold either a third- or fourth-order Fresnel lens. A fourth-order Fresnel lens, designed by French physicist Augustin Fresnel, was the one that was chosen to be mounted at the top of the tower. Encased in brass, a single oil lamp projected a warning beam out onto Lake Erie. The fourth-order lens was designed to be visible thirteen to sixteen miles out on the lake. The light's signature was two red flashes and four white flashes during its one-minute, 360-degree turn. Due to this, the lighthouse soon came to be known as Presque Isle's Flash Light. Its official name was Presque Isle Light Station, although most Erie residents and ship captains immediately began calling it the Flash Light.

The Presque Isle Light Station was officially completed on July 1, 1873, and the light station commenced operation on July 12, 1873. Charles Waldo, the first keeper of the light station, wrote this first entry in his daily log: "This is a new station, and a light will be exhibited for the first time tonight. There was one visitor." Just two days later, Waldo commented in the log that the light itself was working well, but the turning machinery was not and would need some additional work.

At the time of construction, the lighthouse keeper's quarters consisted of a bedroom, dining area, kitchen and summer kitchen on the main floor and three bedrooms and a drying room on the second floor. Beneath the dwelling were located a cistern and a cellar. A sunroom on the northwest corner was added at a later date. At the bottom of the tower was a small service room. The keeper used this room during his nightly tending of the light. It was originally called the "oil room." The keeper was permitted to keep only a single night's oil in this room to use each evening.

The interior of the residence reflected a typical nineteenth-century French architectural design with rounded corners and handcrafted woodwork. Because of the problem of delivery of material to the site, much of the wood for the interior was milled from trees near the station. Two small, potbellied, coal-burning stoves heated the lighthouse, and all cooking was done on a large, wood-burning stove.

In addition to the lighthouse itself, the grounds contained a barn, privies, a storage building for equipment and an oil shed. The oil shed was a brick and metal building located north of the lighthouse where whale oil was stored. Until the lighthouse was electrified, the Lighthouse Service would supply the station with whale oil, kerosene, diesel or other fuels to power the light or generators. It would also bring the keeper and his family food staples twice a year. The flammable materials were stored away from the lighthouse to reduce the risk of fire in the tower and residence.

For over forty years after the opening of the lighthouse, all water for use by the keeper and his family was obtained from a hand-pumped well located on the south side of the dwelling. It was 1957 before the lighthouse finally stopped using outhouses on the property. As you might guess from the preceding descriptions, the life of a keeper and his family was more than a bit rough. Work at the lighthouse was constant and hard. Also, life

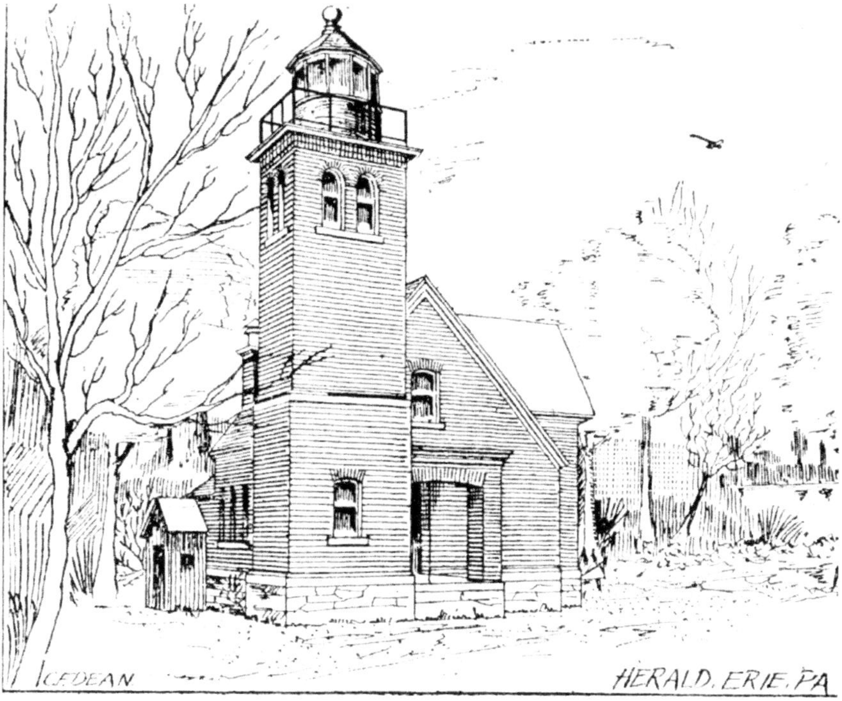

THE FLASH LIGHT-HOUSE.

1888 Erie, Penna. Illustrated (Jeff Kidder Collection)

A drawing of Presque Isle Light Station by J. Kidder. *From the 2007 Presque Isle Lighthouse study report. Pennsylvania DCNR files.*

was lonely and isolated. In the early years, at certain times of the year, fresh food was a problem. The Lighthouse Service and, later, the Coast Guard sent a supply tender to the lighthouse on a regular basis, except for winter supply visits, which were not possible. This led to a short supply of certain foods and other stocks needed at the lighthouse. It is interesting to look at the list of food items annually supplied per person for light stations from 1883 to 1900. That list included the following: beef, two hundred pounds; pork, one hundred pounds; flour, one barrel; rice, twenty-five pounds; beans, ten gallons; potatoes, four bushels; onions, one bushel; sugar, fifty pounds; coffee, twenty-four pounds; vinegar, four gallons; pickles, twenty pounds; cod fish, forty pounds; and corned beef, sixty pounds.

Gathering information from the daily light keepers' logs, I found there were times when it could be a week or more when no visitors came to Presque

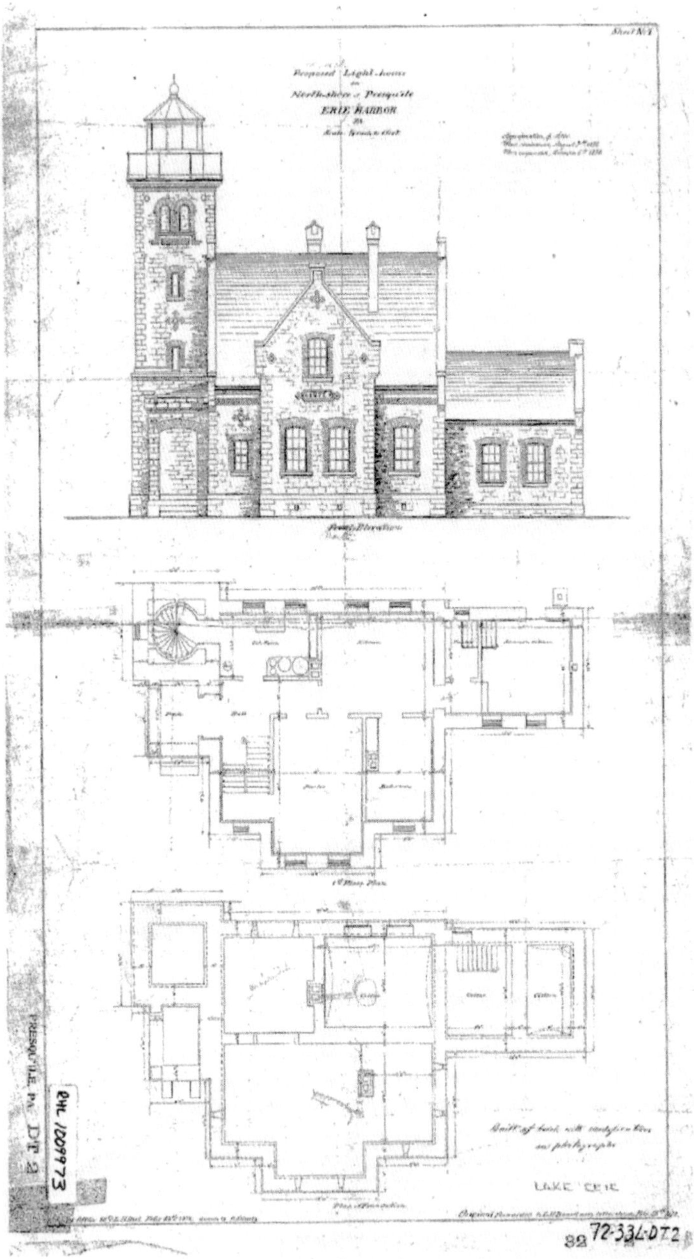

1873 original design drawing (National Archives)

Presque Isle Light Station's final floor plan. *Courtesy of the Pennsylvania DCNR files.*

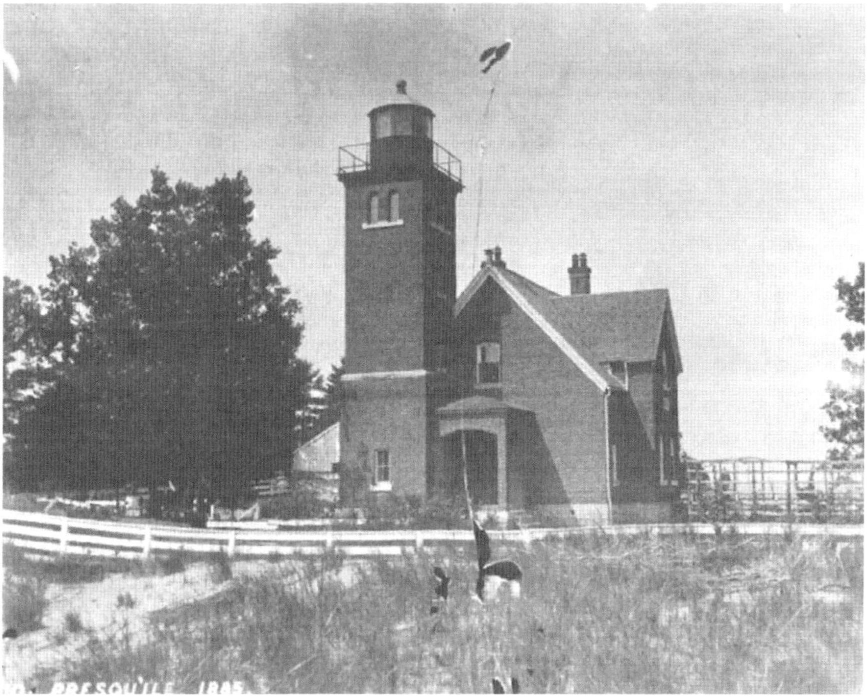

Presque Isle Light Station, 1885. *Courtesy of the Pennsylvania DCNR files.*

Isle to visit the lighthouse. The first keeper, Charles Waldo, who kept the job just over seven years, wrote in his log, "This station is the loneliest place on earth." The second keeper lasted only eight days because his wife and two children, upon seeing the isolated nature of the Presque Isle Light Station, refused to move there and left Erie the very next day without him. It was not until 1892, and five keepers later, that anyone would last more than three years in the position at the Presque Isle Light Station.

Of course, part of the problem was that the position paid just $520 per year and required that the light be kept burning every night from April 1 to the end of November most years. The keeper and his family were responsible for the maintenance and preservation of the tower, residence, grounds, outbuildings and equipment on the property. The keeper was also required to respond to shipwrecks and other emergencies. They were able to occasionally, usually in the off-season, leave the lighthouse for short trips; however, they were required to provide a qualified replacement to cover in their absence.

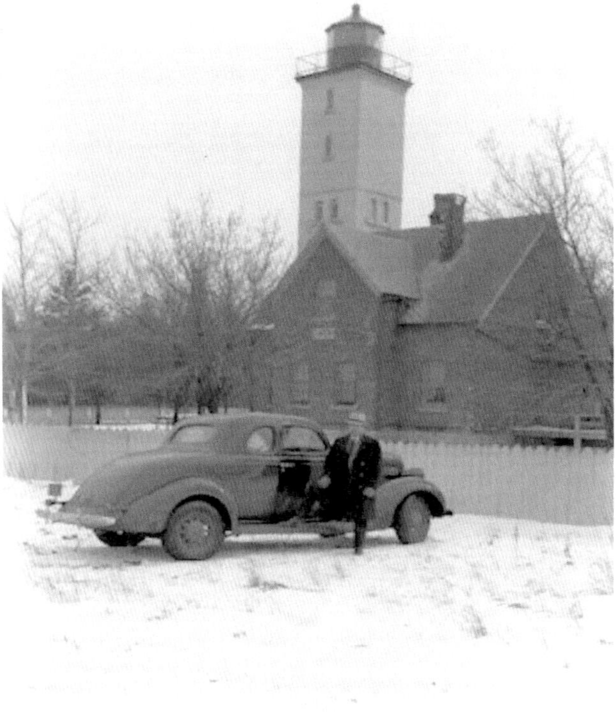

A light keeper and a car at Presque Isle Light Station in the early 1900s. *Courtesy of the Pennsylvania DCNR files.*

Ensuring proper operation of the light required keepers to climb the tower about every one and a half to two hours and clean the lens if necessary, make sure that it was functioning properly, refuel the burner or burners and reset the weight chains. This went on from before sunset to one hour after sunrise each day. During the early years of the light station, it was noted by the keepers and ship captains that the nearby trees and their leaves sometimes partially obscured the view of the light beam. Both suggested that some of the trees be removed. This was done in 1876 when seven large trees were removed.

Nearly all families at the lighthouse had children. In fact, in 1876, Waldo's wife, Mary, gave birth there to a baby girl, who was the first child known to be born on Presque Isle. Many children have called the lighthouse home over the years. That includes families of official keepers, park employees and managers and even some families that agreed to live there to monitor lighthouse operations once the light itself was automated.

Before the roads came to Presque Isle, keepers and their families had to travel to and from the station by boat across the bay to get medical supplies

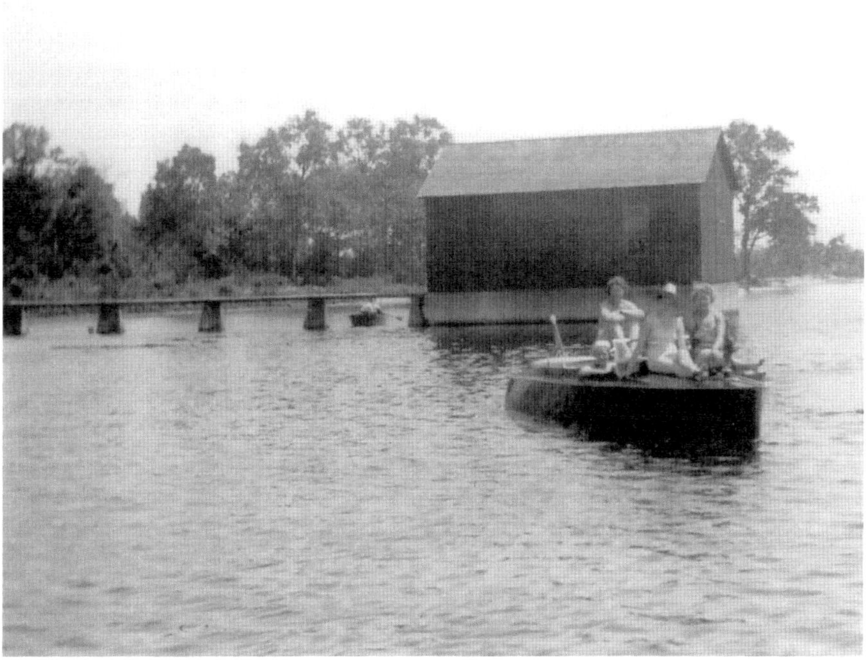

The keeper's boathouse on Misery Bay. *Courtesy of the Pennsylvania DCNR files.*

or treatment, buy common everyday supplies and even go to school or church. In order to go to school, the children would walk to the boathouse or, at times, to the Life-Saving Service Station, and men from the service would row them to and from town. In the winter, the men would walk them across on the ice. Life was not easy for the light keepers and their families.

In 1882, the characteristic of the light was changed from fixed white varied with red flashes to flashing red and white at intervals of ten seconds. Again, at the same time, minor repairs were made in the lantern room and tower. Inspectors, during these early years, thought that the light station was always one of the best kept within their district. In the same year, the keeper, a few fishermen and ship captains complained that the light was now having new visual competition from the many natural gas wells that were burning off excess gas on the shoreline near Massassauga Point at the head of the bay. The resort located there burned gas to light the hotel grounds and docks. At the time, much of the neck of Presque Isle was devoid of trees due to recent breaches of the lake into the bay. Hence, the natural gas lights that were burning in the area were visible out into the lake. This caused much confusion to the mariners on Lake Erie. Over the next two years, Mother Nature took care of this problem by closing the breach and letting bushes and trees begin to grow back.

Within just a few years of its opening, it became clear that the light station might need a few changes, as it was developing a major problem. In 1880, it was decided that an additional boathouse was needed in Misery Bay, and the Lighthouse Service approved $500 for this project. At the same time, the path to Misery Bay was again covered with new wooden planks, but this time, it was raised eight inches above the wet and sandy soil.

But the most serious problem was that the shore in front of the light station was rapidly disappearing under the continuous eastward current and wave action of the lake. By 1884, the shoreline had receded over thirty to forty feet. In 1886, a contract was signed to build a substantial jetty of stone-filled cribs four hundred feet long and eight feet wide out into the lake. This jetty was started on July 6, 1886, and was to be completed by September 1 of that year. This was before the fall and winter season commenced. The Lighthouse Service believed this would protect the shore directly in front of the lighthouse.

I must go down to the sea again, to the lonely sea and sky,
And all I ask is a tall ship and a star to steer her by,
And the wheel's kick and the wind's song and the white sail's shaking,
And a grey mist on the sea's face and a grey dawn breaking.
—John Masefield, 1878–1967

The new jetty was built to stand 3 feet above the normal Lake Erie water level. This was a total success; it caused a new 265-foot beach to form to the west of the light in just its first year. An added unexpected benefit was that it also caused the formation of a new 187-foot beach to the east of the jetty. This jetty now allowed the Lighthouse Service to use it to deliver the light station's supplies more safely. While work on the jetty was taking place, a large number of minor repairs were made to the light station itself, including adding new flooring to the oil room.

By 1885, the land around the light station was enclosed with a painted wood fence made up of four horizontal boards with spaces between them. Sometime between 1894 and 1895, the rail fence was replaced with a tight board picket fence with a flat top. This type of fence was installed to protect the station and grounds from the windblown sand. In 1935, it was replaced by a similar fence but with a sawtooth top. The current chainlink fence was installed in 1974 and, at that time, was positioned to enclose a much larger area of land.

After ten years of weather and continuous use, a boardwalk that ran between the dwelling and the barn was replaced. At the same time, three hundred linear feet of the superstructure of the jetty protecting the shoreline in front of the station were raised, restored and leveled to the original height of three feet above water level.

In 1896, it was decided that the range of the light directed out onto Lake Erie needed to be increased from the original thirteen miles to seventeen or more miles. Engineers calculated that the tower would need an additional seventeen feet of height to accomplish this. A contract was put out to bid, and an addition to the tower was added that summer. The new height at the steel balcony was increased to just a little over fifty-seven feet. With the light room included, the light itself was now at a functional sixty-three feet above the beach. The total overall height of the tower to the top of the ventilator ball mechanism was seventy feet. The year after the completion of this extension, the tower bricks were painted white to provide more prominent daytime visual identification for vessels on Lake Erie.

The lighthouse, like most during this period, burned mainly whale oil. In 1898, the lighthouse lamps were converted to burn the cleaner and now more reliable kerosene. This was possible due to the conversion to the new Argand air lamps, which had been installed one year earlier. These lamps now made kerosene much safer to handle and produced much more light without producing as much soot as the Lewis lamp had. The conversion did, however, require the building of a new oil storage shed for the protection of the light, the keeper and his family because kerosene was much more volatile than whale or lard oils.

Over time, many changes and improvements took place at the light station. This included converting the wooden walkway to Misery Bay to concrete, rebuilding the jetty in concrete, electrifying the station in 1924 and adding a fuel oil– or desiel engine–driven electric generator. A telephone line between the Pierhead Light, the Coast Guard station and the Presque Isle Light was added at the same time. Another change—the one that affected the station the most—was the opening of roads on Presque Isle.

Sometime in 1923, a single-lane road was built down the hill leading to Presque Isle, and in 1925, this road was extended to bring visitors to Presque Isle as far as Waterworks Park. This road increased the number of visitors to Presque Isle ten-fold within the first eighteen months. In less than two years, this road was extended to just past the Presque Isle Light Station. It was built on the lake side of the light station. Soon the number of people coming to view and tour the light station grew tremendously. In addition,

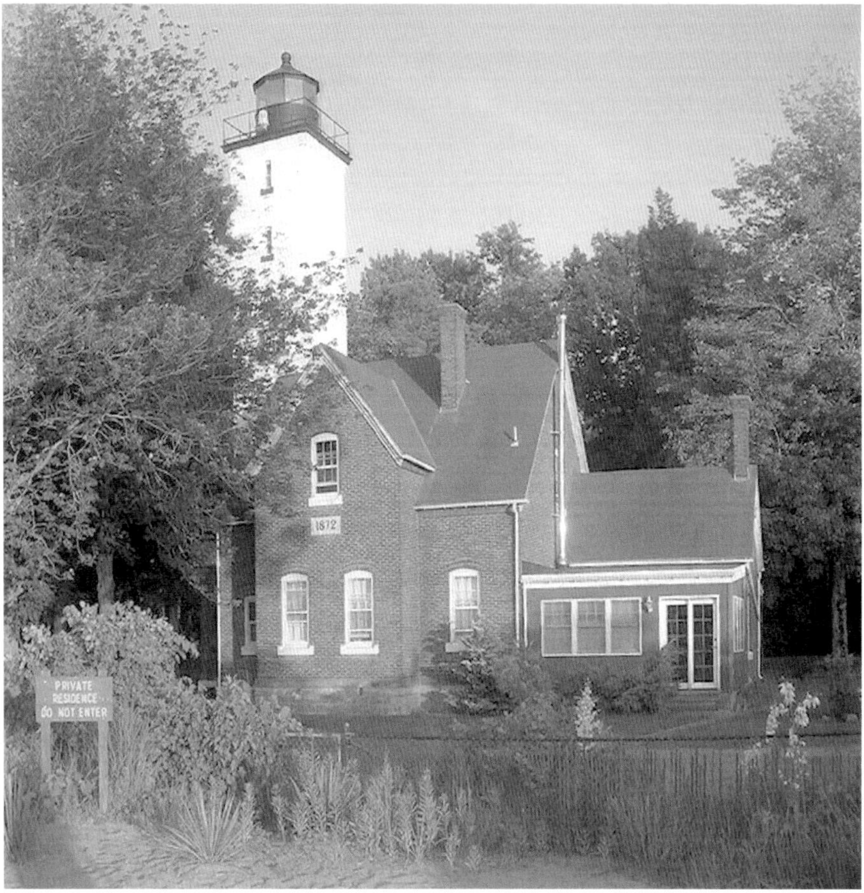

The Presque Isle Light Station in 2011 before the removal of excess and diseased trees. *Author's collection.*

Waterworks Park police, hired by the water department, patrolled the area on horseback for a number of years. In the summer, people visited the light station to picnic on the beach and see the tower. In fact, its popularity grew so much that light keeper Andrew Shaw Jr. decided to retire on August 31, 1927, saying, "Too many blasted people were stopping in to see the light and talk to me." He said he liked the quiet and solitude of the light and could not stand having all the people around because it bothered him tremendously. Soon after his retirement, Frank Huntington was appointed keeper, and he became the longest-serving keeper ever to be at the light station. He did not retire until 1944.

The original site of the lighthouse was 450 feet from the water, but this distance was constantly changing due to storms on the lake and erosion along the shoreline. A small jetty was eventually put in place to help secure the area so that the lighthouse would not be in danger. In fact, the lake was so turbulent that when a road finally came to the area in 1927 and was built between the lighthouse and the water, it took less than twenty years for storms off of Lake Erie to destroy it. A new road south of the lighthouse was built shortly afterward; it is still in use today.

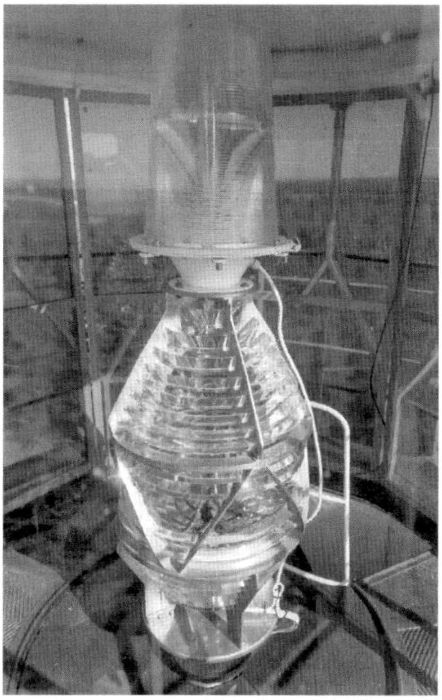

This is a Fresnel lens with an electrical beacon light. *Courtesy of Pennsylvania DCNR files.*

In 1949, the U.S. Coast Guard automated the electrical light that had been originally installed in 1924. During the original conversion to electric, many problems were encountered, so once the light was working properly, there was great reluctance to make any new changes in the light's operation. The change to an automated system went very well though, and even today, the light functions perfectly on a day-to-day basis. It was not until 1962 that the Coast Guard removed the original light with its Fresnel lens and brass movements. A new airport beacon took its place. The Fresnel lens was sent to a Coast Guard museum. Unfortunately, no one has ever been able to find where the lens actually went, and it is still missing.

As years went by, the ownership, uses and control of the light station changed many times. During the next forty years, many additions, remodelings and other changes took place at the light station. One constant factor during this time was that the light station was never open to the public. This bothered many citizens within the Erie community, and soon a quiet behind-the-scenes movement for change in governmental policies began to grow.

In 1983, the light station was entered into the National Register of Historic Places, and from that date forward, a much clearer path to better and public use of the property began to finally seem possible. This improved and more sensible use as a historic landmark would eventually lead to opening the light station to the public.

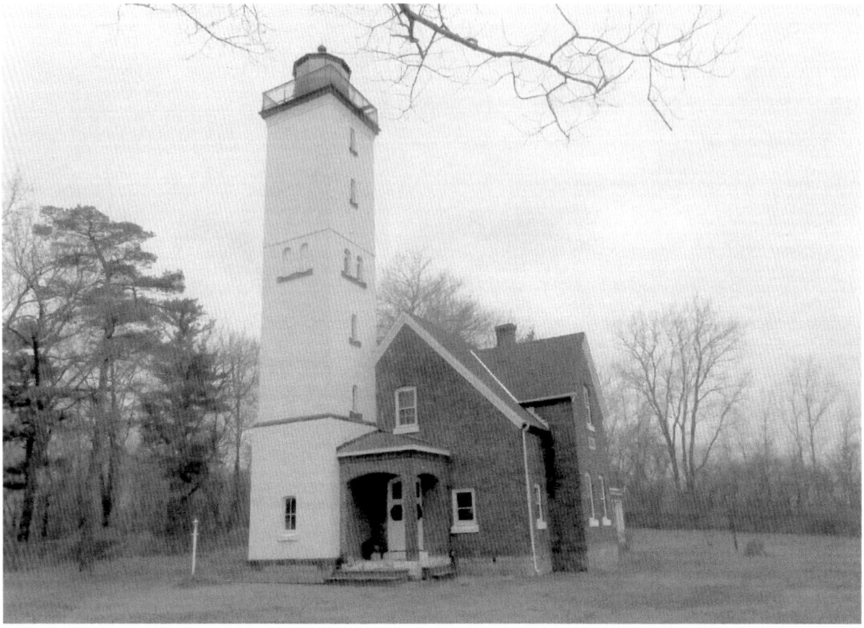

Presque Isle Light Station, 2014. *Author's collection.*

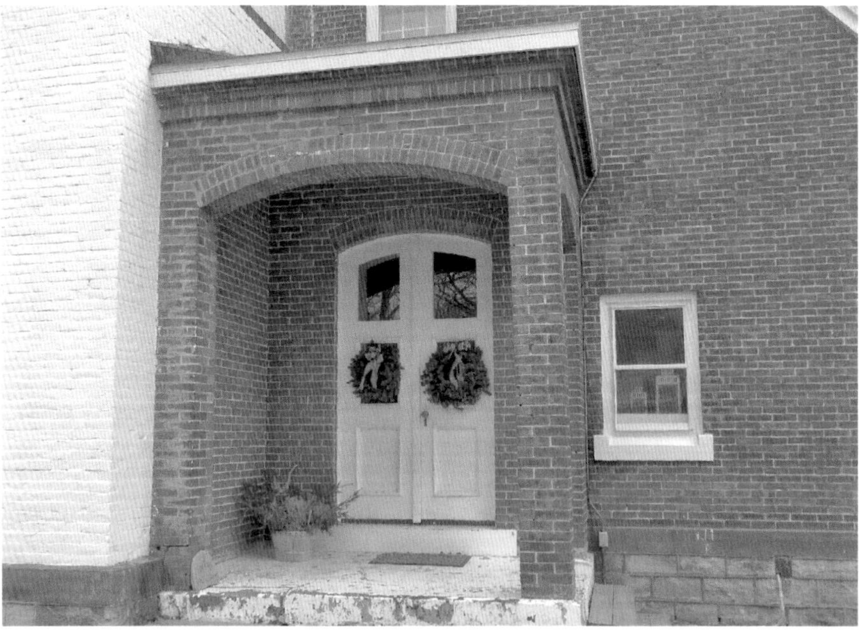

Christmas wreaths on the main door of the Presque Isle Light Station in 2014. *Author's collection.*

The second enormous step in this process was taken in 1998 when the administrator of general services for the United States of America deeded the light station to the Pennsylvania Department of Conservation and Natural Resources. While the property was still a state park manager's home and the manager still occupied the property for a number of years, there was now a much greater possibility that sometime in the not-too-distant future, the light station could become the historic landmark it should be and be opened to the public.

Two key events happened in the fall of 2014. The first was that the manager living in the light station and his family moved to a new home just outside the park's boundary, and the property was vacant for the first time in many years. The other was that a new nonprofit 501C(3) organization named the Presque Isle Light Station was formed and approved by the IRS.

Once this was done, the nonprofit worked with the Department of Conversation and Natural Resources and the governor's office in Harrisburg to negotiate the terms of a thirty-five-year lease of the property. The intention was to restore the light to the look it had in the early 1900s and open it to the public for educational and history-based tours and events. First-year plans for the historic station included being open on weekends and holidays starting in the summer of 2015. The staff will conduct educational tours and viewings. At first, this will be only during the summer months, and as time and staff allow, it eventually will be expanded to be open seven days a week. That process is now well underway. Taking the Presque Isle Light Station back to the early 1900s should help preserve some of the great moments and experiences of the past of this special place.

8

THE LIGHT KEEPER AND HIS LIFE

Wouldn't living and working in a lighthouse have been wonderful? To many people, this must seem like the ideal job. You could have taken daily walks on the beach, lived a fascinating life in a very romantic place, picnicked with friends on the beach and been surrounded by nature at its best. Every day, deer, shorebirds, foxes and raccoons would play in your front yard. If you had been the lighthouse keeper, you might have enjoyed all of the above before spending your evenings in the lantern room atop your lighthouse. Your job then would be trimming the wicks and maintaining watch out on the lake for ships and boats in trouble. What a great place the lantern room must have been back then. You could take a cup of coffee and a book up with you and begin your evening just watching the shorebirds play in the light's beacon, sipping your coffee and keeping up with your reading.

I think that many people believe that working at a lighthouse must surely have been moderately easy work. Most people have the idea that lighthouses were places for hobbies, reading, relaxing and walking the sandy beaches looking for colorful beach glass. I read in a quotation book many years ago that Albert Einstein suggested that the development of a great mind might be more readily accomplished if one were sent to live in the peace and solitude of a lighthouse. This might be true as long as he or she was just a visitor and not a keeper. This hypothetical look back at the glamour and intrigue of lighthouse life sure seems wonderful, except it was far from true.

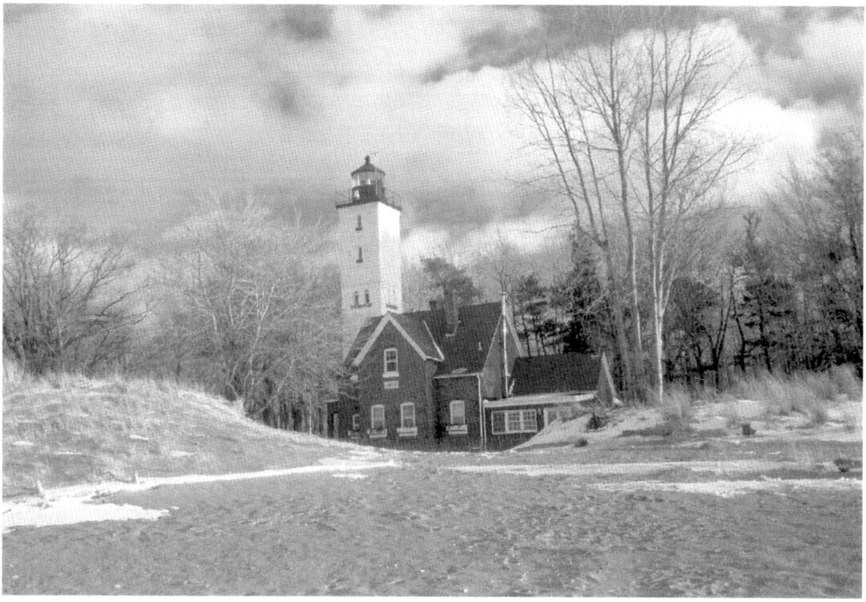

Winter at Presque Isle Light Station. *Author's collection.*

Although there have been small glimpses into the lives of the lighthouse keepers in other places in this book, this chapter will provide more thorough details and insights of their time spent on the job.

Being a lighthouse keeper was definitely not an easy job. The actual duties varied by lighthouse, and in most cases, location played an important part in determining those duties. The lighthouses in Erie and on the Great Lakes, in general, have always had shorter seasons than those located in the southern United States or on the ocean shorelines. On the Great Lakes, winter closed down many lighthouses, yet most were still year-round jobs for keepers and their families. Starting in 1881, the keepers' lives and duties were governed by a small book called *Instructions to Employees of the United States Lighthouse Service*. This book had several updates over the years. The job of the lighthouse keeper was very important because many lives depended on the lighthouse and its keeper to keep them safe. The keeper himself depended on this manual to successfully carry out his job in a detailed and prescribed manner. The very first duty set forth in this manual was: "The keeper is responsible for the care and management of the light, and for the station in general. He must enforce a careful attention to duty on the part of his assistants; and assistants are strictly enjoined to render prompt obedience to his lawful orders." The first four pages of this manual list thirty-three separate general orders that all keepers were to follow.

The most important part of a keeper's duty was to always keep the light operating according to a schedule determined by local conditions. Usually, this was from early dusk to one hour past dawn. Yet during poor weather conditions—like severe thunderstorms, gales and hurricanes—that could mean twenty-four hours a day or until the storm was over. Keepers were given huge leeway in deciding when the light was needed in these cases. One of the most important general orders in the manual set the times of operation quite clearly: "Lights must be exhibited punctually at sunset and kept lighted at full intensity until sunrise, when light may be extinguished and the apparatus put in order without delay for relighting." Basically, that meant that even after dousing the light at sunrise, the keeper's work was not done yet. He must get the light ready to light the next evening by checking the wick, cleaning the lenses and restocking the oil or kerosene. These responsibilities could take at least three or more hours.

When not in the lighthouse, the keeper was expected to survey the weather; beach conditions; tides, if any; and the exterior condition of the lighthouse. If the lighthouse had a lifeboat or any other vessel assigned to the station, it was to be regularly checked. In the case of the Presque Isle Light Station, the boat on Misery Bay was to be checked every other day. All light station keepers were also required to keep a daily log of all activity at the light. This became the station's official logbook for the keeper's future reference and the lighthouse inspector's use during ongoing inspections. The keeper was also to keep an accurate daily log of all expenses incurred at the light.

Most lighthouse keepers were married and had children, so the families tended to work together on some of the light keeper's duties. Most times, these shared duties included maintaining the grounds, planting and tending a vegetable garden and cleaning the tower and living quarters. Some of the keepers' wives also helped their husbands keep a full inventory of supplies needed for all areas of the light station.

In 1883, uniforms were introduced to lighthouses across the United States. By 1884, all keepers were expected to begin their day dressed in one of the official uniforms of the Lighthouse Service. The dress uniform consisted of blue pants, a vest, a suit jacket and a hat. In most cases, these uniforms were made of good quality wool. The keeper, not the Lighthouse Service, purchased these uniforms. A uniform, whether dress or common, had to be worn at all times while on duty. If a keeper was found not wearing the uniform or not wearing it properly, he could be fined or dismissed. A uniform was to be worn even when working with oil or kerosene. However, when cleaning in the lantern room and around the lens, the service required he wear a smock as was described earlier in this book. This was not just to protect the uniform but also to protect the lenses. The Lighthouse Service provided the smocks. Considering the cost of the uniforms, most keepers used the smock quite often. Even today, in many lighthouse museums, linen smocks are used to keep the Fresnel lenses clean and free of damage.

There was also another, less formal uniform called the common work uniform. It could be worn at times when the dress uniform was not required. The Lighthouse Service printed a fourteen-page pamphlet issued to all personnel that described and illustrated both uniforms. It clearly indicated when and why a keeper should wear each type of uniform. No deviation from these instructions was permitted. The common work uniform was made of a dungaree-type material and had shirts or blouses and trousers or overalls. A conical, flattop navy blue hat went with this version of the uniform. On work details, keepers could wear tan or black shoes with only black socks. Many light keepers in southern areas complained about having to wear only black socks due to the summer heat, yet this policy never changed.

The keeper's job included much more than just keeping the lenses clean and lit. It also meant keeping the lantern room windows clear and clean in all kinds of weather conditions, including rain, snow, sleet or ice. Sometimes the keeper was forced to clean windows in gale force winds and heavy snow and ice. All keepers knew that this was exactly the type of weather when ships and their crews needed the lighthouse most. That is why the keepers were always more diligent during the worst weather.

While much of what keepers were required to do became routine, as always, they were prepared to deal with unexpected problems. The single item that worried the keeper and his family most was fire. Much of what he dealt with on his job involved lubricating oils, paints and varnish, whale oil, kerosene, coal and firewood. All of these were stored in the area of the lighthouse, never within it. In fact, there were definite limits covering just how much whale oil or kerosene could be brought into the lighthouse's lantern room at a time for use at the light itself.

Fire buckets painted bright red and filled with water were positioned within the lighthouse and residence at all times. Some lighthouses also spotted buckets of sand near the living quarters' cooking and heating stoves. All of these buckets were required to be checked daily. Most lighthouses required monthly fire drills. Any emergency that took place at the lighthouse required a detailed report to be sent to the district

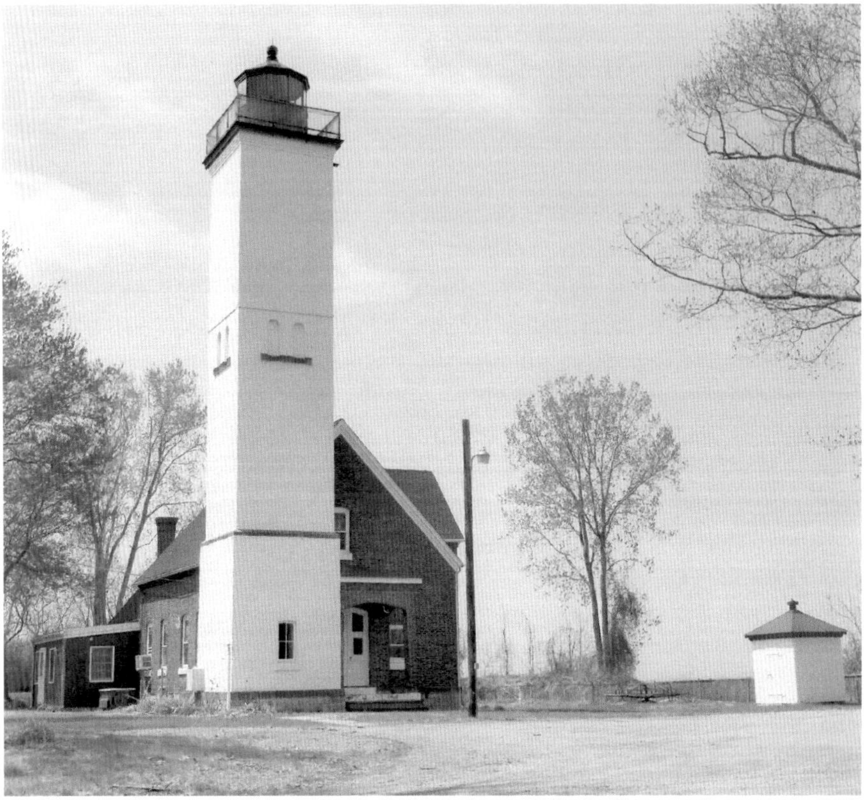

The Presque Isle Light Station in the fall of 2014 after the removal of diseased trees. *Author's collection.*

supervisor covering what happened and the keeper's response to the emergency. In addition to this report, the keeper was required to prepare and send nine other reports to the supervisor on a regular schedule. The keeper's job was highly report and paper intensive.

The keeper's position had many and varied requirements, including age, water-related skills, physical ability, civil service requirements, fitness as a boatman in sail and motor in all kinds of weather and the ability to read and write in English. He was to have skills with machinery and mechanical apparatus. For a while, there was a rule that no one over the age of fifty could become a new lighthouse keeper, and at one point, only married men could even apply for the keeper's position. In addition to tending the light and the obligations above, the keeper's duties might have included:

- paint as needed
- make minor repairs
- install and replace equipment
- clean the chimneys, stove and heaters
- conduct tours of the lighthouse and grounds
- explain operation of the light
- have the ability and knowledge to review the lighthouse history
- be able to explain to inspectors and engineers all problems encountered at the lighthouse since their last inspection
- know and practice first aid

At Erie's lighthouses, a long list of keepers have serviced over the years. Following is a complete list of them, when they served and at what lighthouse:

Erie Land Lighthouse

John Bone	1819–1833
Samuel Foster	1833
Robert Kincaide	1833–1841
Griffith Hinton	1841–1845
Eli Webster	1845–1850
Roderick Petion	1850
James W. Miles	1850–1853
Isabel Miles	1853–1854
John Graham	1854–1858
James Fleming	1858
A.C. Landon	1858–1861
John Goading	1861–1864
George Desmond	1864–1871
A.J. Fargo	1871–1881
George Miller	1885–1899

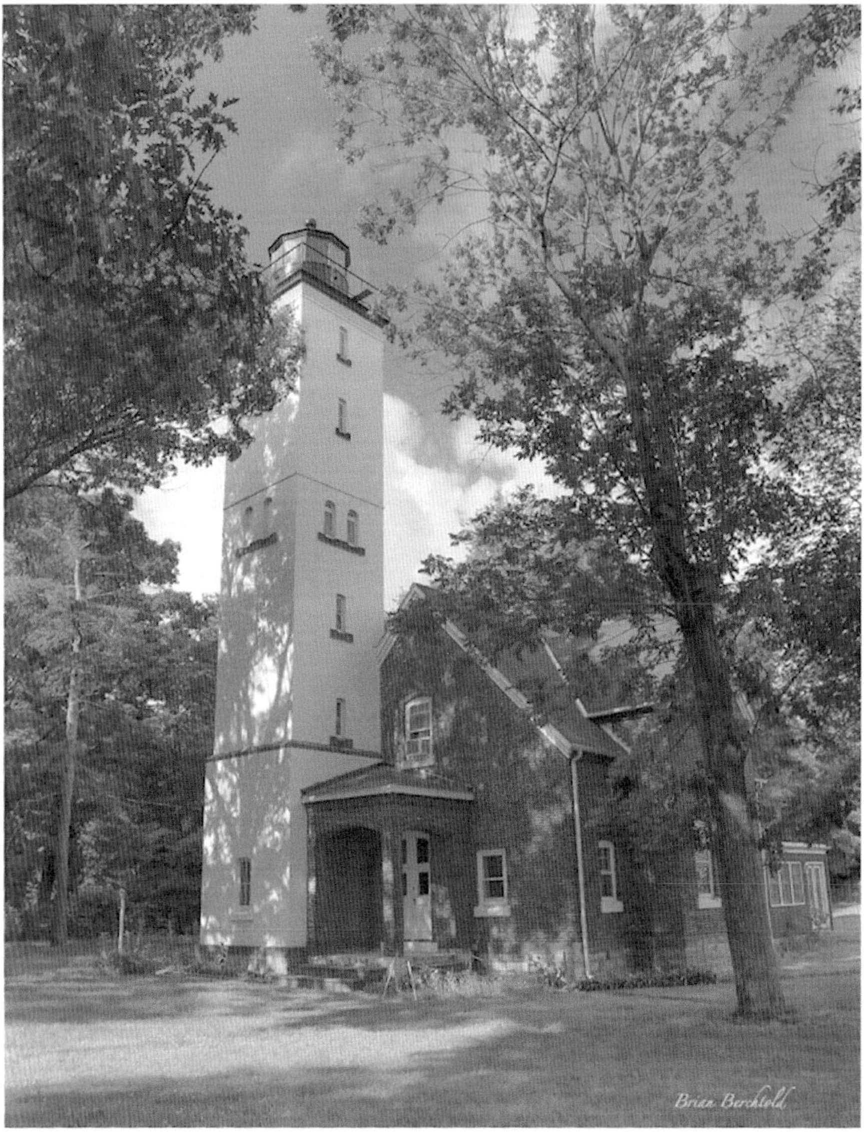

A spring 2015 view of the Presque Isle Light Station. *Courtesy of Brian Berchtold.*

Presque Isle North Pierhead Light Station

Head

Samuel Foster	1835–1837
William Kane	1837–1841
Ben Fleming	1841–1845
Leonard Vaugh	1845–1850
Rubin Field	1850
John Hess	1850–1853
William Downs	1853–1854
Leonard Vaugh	1854–1861
George Bone	1861–1863
Richard Burke	1863–1869
Frank Henry	1869–1884
Charles Coyle	1884–1889
Robert Hunter	1890–1901
Thomas Wilkins	1901–1909
Robert Allen	1909–1935
Walter Korwek	1935–1946
Earl Malloch	1946–

Assistants

Francis Arnold	1908–1909
Frank Huntington	1918–1926
Eugene Liebel	1930–1933
Frank Huntington	1933–1944

Presque Isle Light Station

Charles Waldo	1873–1880
Orrin McAllister	1880
George Town	1880–1883
Clark McCole	1883–1886
Lewis Vannatta	1886–1891
Lewis Walrose	1891–1892
Thomas Wilkins	1892–1901
Andrew Shaw	1901–1927
Frank Huntington	1927–1944

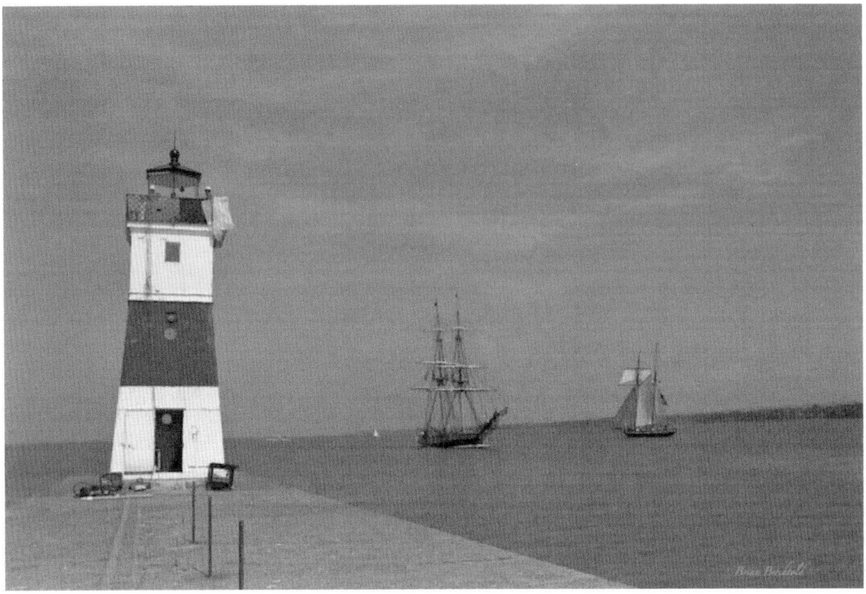

A 2010 photograph of the flagship *Niagara* entering the Erie harbor and passing the North Pierhead Light. *Courtesy of Brian Berchtold.*

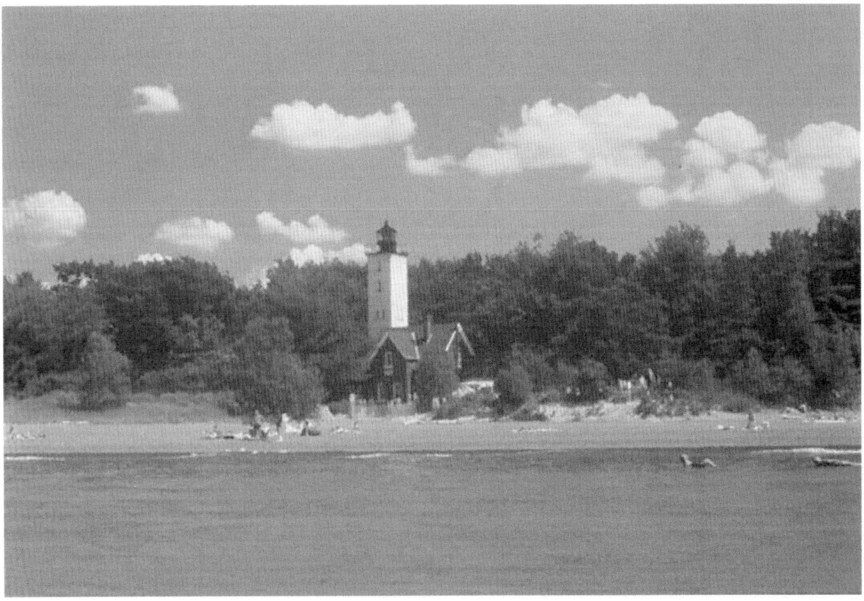

A spring 2015 view of the Presque Isle Light Station. *Courtesy of Brian Berchtold.*

Each and every one of these lighthouse keepers had a story or two to tell, even poor Orrin McAllister. He lasted on the job just two or three days and resigned and left Erie after eight days. His family refused to join him on Presque Isle when they discovered its lonely and desolate location. The fact that to get to their home they would have to be rowed across the bay or walk on the ice in the winter was the final straw for Mrs. McAllister. She never visited the lighthouse and left Erie long before her husband. Some keepers and their families hated the loneliness that came with life at the Presque Isle Light Station, while others, like Andrew Shaw, loved the fact that he saw no one for days on end.

Even the original Presque Isle Light Station has some stories to tell. As you learned in the chapter about the first lighthouse on the lake, the Erie Land Lighthouse, John Bone and his family of seven moved into the three-room keeper's dwelling when the lighthouse first opened. Mrs. Bone gave birth to another boy just two years later. To add a little more to the crowding at the light, the eldest daughter, then twenty-two, married, and she and her husband also moved in with the family for a short time.

Even today, lighthouses remain an enduring symbol of human courage, bravery and faithfulness. Although modern-day improvements

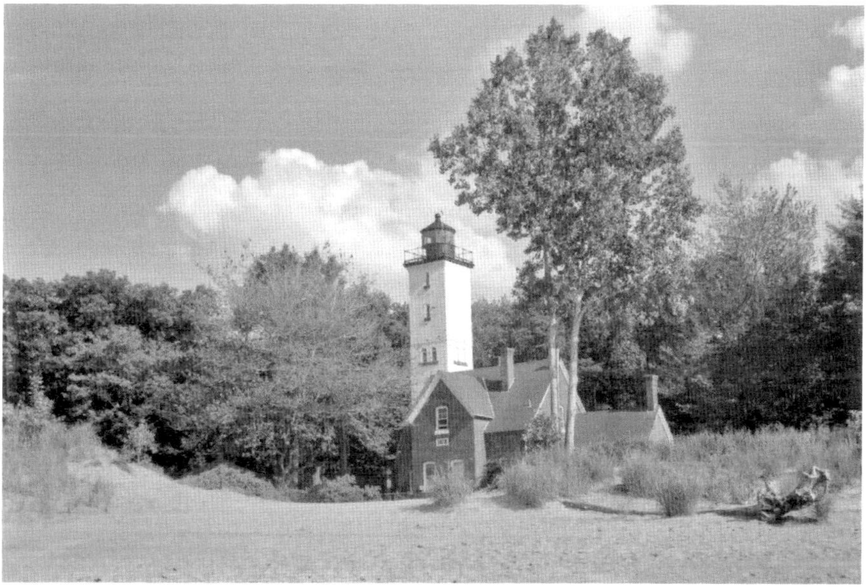

A 1996 summer view of the Presque Isle Light Station from the beach before the formation of large beachside sand dunes. *Author's collection.*

in navigation, expertise and equipment have made many of the world's tough old towers obsolete and timeworn, there has been a resurgence and growing concern for their historic preservation. Could there a better place to come down to than the beach in front of the Presque Isle Light Station? You can just relax and sit among the dunes on a beautiful afternoon and watch the lake and the birds that play in the area. I see many people as they wander around the grounds of the Presque Isle Light Station, and just from the looks on their faces, I can tell they still cling to the romantic and magical illusions that life at a lighthouse evokes in many people's minds. Over the years, I have discovered that when it comes to lighthouses, many people just cannot grow up. They cannot let the reality of lighthouse operations interfere with their youthful dreams of the solitude, peace and leisure that lighthouse life seemed to offer.

From the Pharos to our marvelous Erie lighthouses, these iconic structures have always stood isolated and alone, protecting brave mariners at sea. From the first bonfires on the beaches or lights kindled by whale oil, kerosene and electricity, the lighthouse has eternally been a sign of hope and confidence. Today, lighthouses remain an object of mystic beauty and history in a world that all too often looks only to the future. My advice is to visit them often and enjoy their special place and time where hard work and adventure reigned alongside solitude and peace.

There is pleasure in the pathless woods;
There is rapture on the lonely shore;
There is society where none intruded;
By the deep sea, and music in its roar:
I love not man the less, but Nature more.

—*Lord Byron (1788–1824)*

BIBLIOGRAPHY

Bates, Samuel P. *History of Erie County, Pennsylvania*. Chicago: Warner, Beers and Co., 1884.

Beers, J.B. *History of the Great Lakes*. Chicago: L.H. Beers and Co., 1899.

Brandon, Loretta. *Lightkeeper's Legacy: A Personal History of Presque Isle*. Erie, PA: Erie County Historical Society, 1997.

Crompton, Samuel Willard, and Michael Rhein. *The Ultimate Book of Lighthouses*. San Diego, CA: Thunder Bay Press, 2001.

Department of the Navy. Naval History and Heritage Command. *Battle of Lake Erie: Building the Fleet in the Wilderness*. Washington, D.C.: Naval Historical Foundation, 1979.

De Wire, Elinor. *Guardians of the Lights*. Sarasota, FL: Pineapple Press, Inc., 1995.

Dobbins, Daniel. Papers. 1800–49. Microfilm. Buffalo History Museum Research Library, Buffalo, NY.

Dobbins, W.W. *Battle of Lake Erie*. Erie, PA: Ashby Printing Co., 1876.

Fredricksen, John C., ed. *Surgeon of the Lakes*. Erie, PA: Erie County Historical Society, 2000.

Frew, David. *Perry's Lake Erie Fleet: After the Glory*. Charleston, SC: The History Press, 2012.

Graham, Donald. *Keepers of the Light*. Madeira Park, BC: Harbour Publishing Ltd., 1985.

Hickey, Donald R. *187 Things You Should Know About the War of 1812*. Baltimore, MD: Baltimore Historical Society, 2012.

Ilservich, Robert D. *Daniel Dobbins: Frontier Mariner*. Erie, PA: Erie County Historical Society, 1993.

Levitt, Theresa. *A Short Bright Flash*. New York: W.W. Norton & Co., 2014.

Merrill, John. *Becoming a Surfman in 1938*. www.jacksjoint.com, 2014.

Muller, Mary M. *A Town at Presque Isle*. Erie, PA: Erie County Historical Society, 1991.

National Park Service, U.S. Coast Guard and Department of Defense. *Historic Lighthouse Preservation Handbook*. Washington, D.C.: U.S. Government Printing Office, 2009.

Nelson, S.B. *Historical Reference Book of Erie County, Pennsylvania*. Erie, PA: S.B. Nelson, 1896.

Noble, Dennis L., and Coast Guard Public Affairs Staff, Great Lakes. *A Brief History of U.S. Coast Guard Operations*. Washington, D.C.: U.S. Government Printing Office, 2010.

Pennsylvania Department of Conservation and Natural Resources, Bureau of State Parks. PA: *Historic Structure Report*, 2007.

Reed, John Elmer. *History of Erie County*. Columbus, OH: Historical Publishing Co., 1925.

Rosenberg, Max. *The Building of Perry's Fleet on Lake Erie*. Harrisburg, PA: Commonwealth of Pennsylvania Historical and Museum Commission, 1997.

Ross, Alan. *The Lure of Lighthouse*. Nashville, TN: Walnut Grove Press, 1999.

Sanford, Laura. *The History of Erie County*. N.p.: self-published, 1894.

U.S. Army Corps of Engineers. *History of Erie Harbor, PA*. Buffalo, NY: U.S. Army Corps of Engineers, 1941.

U.S. Coast Guard. *Instructions to Light-Keepers*. Washington, D.C.: Government Printing Office, 1881.

———. *Life-Saving Report Fiscal Year 1884*. Washington, D.C.: Government Printing Office, 1884.

Weber, Mark T. *History of the U.S. Life-Saving Station, Erie, PA*. Erie, PA: Erie Maritime Museum, 2005.

INDEX

L

N

P

R

S

U

W

ABOUT THE AUTHOR

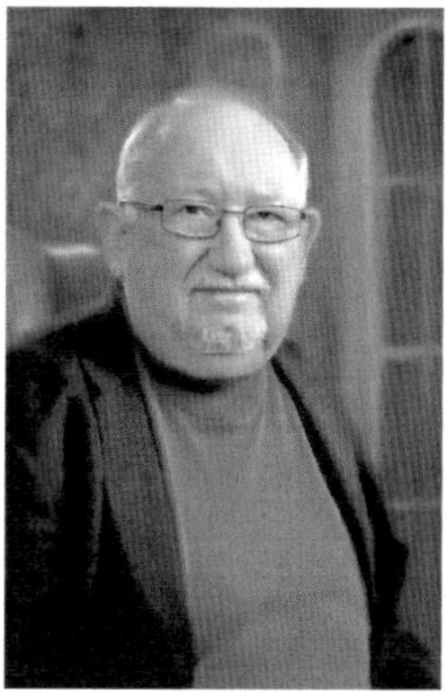

Eugene H. Ware is a native of Erie, Pennsylvania, and he and his wife, Nancy, have lived three blocks from the entrance to Presque Isle State Park for over fifty years. His and Nancy's interest in the park comes from daily year-round visits to the park. He and his wife have three children—Pam, Paula and Marcia—plus four grandchildren and two grcat-grandchildrcn.

A financial consultant for over fifty years, Gene worked at a local bank for thirty years and as an independent financial planning and investment advisor for twenty-two years. He and his wife owned and operated an art gallery and frame shop for over twenty years.

Gene has served on many local nonprofit boards, acting as president of seven of them. He serves as past president of the Presque Isle Partnership, the Sight Center of Northwest Pennsylvania, the Workforce Investment Board, the Northwestern Pennsylvania Humane Society, the Erie Jacees and the Sales and Marketing Association of Erie. He currently is president of the Friends of Tom Ridge Environmental Center and treasurer of the newly formed Presque Isle Light Station. He is also a sustaining member of the Historical Society of Erie County.

He is an avid photographer and writer, having published five prior books with Presque Isle as their subject. His newest, *Natural Impressions of Presque Isle*

State Park, is a coffee-table book with over 125 color photographs of the park. He is a member of Pennwriters, a statewide writers' group. He regularly speaks at many functions about his favorite topic, Presque Isle State Park.

Recently, the local newspaper established a blog that is entitled "Presque Isle—A Place for All Seasons." The blog has been very successful and readership much higher than the newspaper expected. Gene writes two new entries each week on the blog and includes many pictures of his own as well as those from other photographers and friends of the park.

He hopes that his writing will bring back fond memories of Presque Isle and inspire others to contact him with new and different information and pictures of Presque Isle's bygone years and also their more recent experiences on Presque Isle. He views these books and his blog as just a beginning of his exploration of Presque Isle.